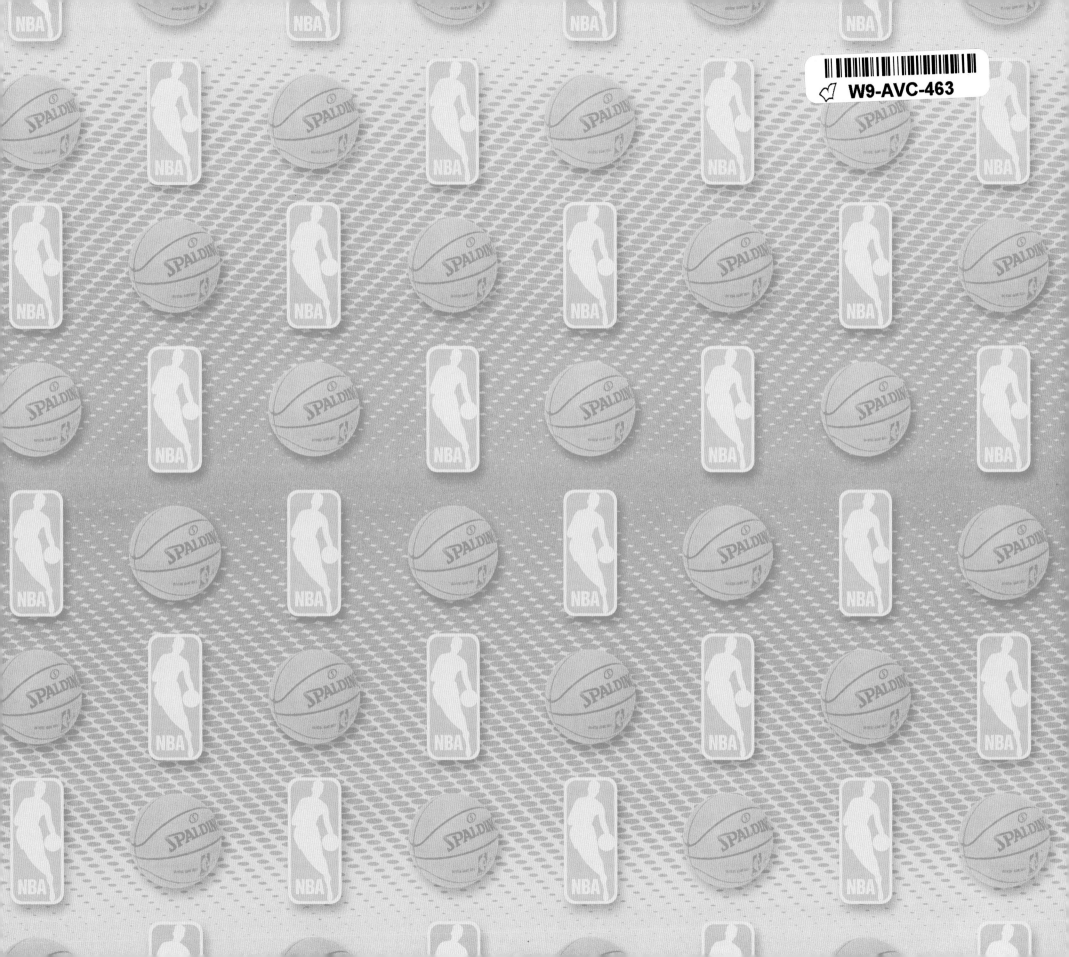

The NBA's Greatest Teams

ROLAND LAZENBY

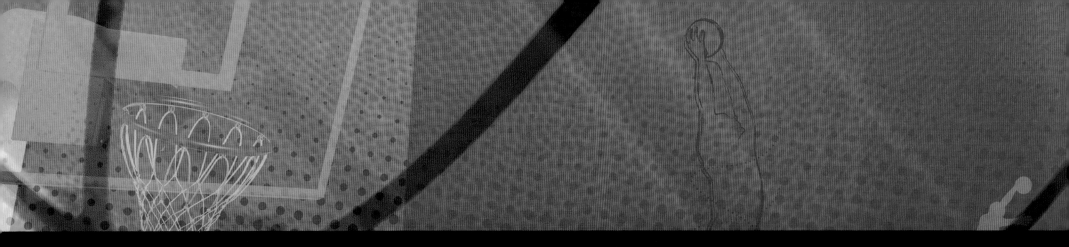

The NBA's Greatest Teams

Whitman
Publishing, LLC
PUBLISHING SINCE 1934

ISBN: 0794833780
Printed and assembled in China

Note: All removable documents and memorabilia in this book are replicas and not originals themselves.

To view other products by Whitman Publishing, please visit **www.Whitman.com**.

TABLE OF CONTENTS

THE SUM OF ALL THE PARTS

OK, it's a little odd. The NBA, long the domain of star players and star power, is allowing me to write a book celebrating the league's greatest teams from eight decades of competition.

Yes, this book also showcases the great stars who have driven the interest in pro basketball over the years. But as Hall of Famer Tex Winter so often likes to point out, it's the team success, the mysterious sum of all the parts, that allows the stars to make their mark.

"In the final analysis, it's a team game," Winter once told me. "Always has been. Always will be. And the greatness of these star players is mostly based on what their teams achieve."

Thus, it's only fitting that this *NBA's Greatest Teams* book is dedicated to all the people — the role players, sixth men, defensive specialists — who have made the sacrifices that helped their teams to greatness. At the 2011 NBA Finals, I consulted with some of the game's greatest players, coaches and front-office executives, and this book is the sum of their opinions on the 20 greatest NBA teams ever.

It's only appropriate that the greatest team on the list — the 1962-63 Boston Celtics — sported a roster filled with future Hall of Famers, yet none of them averaged even 20 points per game.

"We ran things, we moved without the ball," explained Hall of Famer Tommy Heinsohn. "If we were open, we got the ball. We played basketball. ... We were all involved in how we played. It was nobody that felt they had to defer to anybody else. We were a team. I mean we never had a guy who was a top-10 scorer."

Even so, some might say we've gone out on a limb in picking the 1962-63 Celtics to top the list of the greatest NBA teams. Led by the great Bill Russell, they won 11 titles in 13 seasons (and made a dozen trips to the championship round).

With such dominance, they made a tremendous impression on generations of NBA players, despite the fact that the Celtics didn't compete in an era when NBA games were widely broadcast.

Kareem Abdul-Jabbar recalled seeing them frequently as an adolescent in his native New York because of the doubleheaders the NBA staged in the Big Apple in the 1950s and '60s.

"I grew up watching the Celtics," Abdul-Jabbar once explained to me. "I grew up watching Bill Russell's teams. That's how I learned to play the game. I watched them. My coach in high school coached that style, so I always saw them as being exemplary of the way the game should be played."

Supposedly the knock against those Celtics is that they couldn't compete against the teams of today with bigger, stronger, faster athletes. Former Celtic Satch Sanders disputes that by pointing out that Russell's Celtics were simply the most "blood-thirsty" team of all time.

"We would still be winners," Sanders said told me on the eve of his 2011 induction into the Basketball Hall of Fame. "Old-timers never die. We always win. But we'd have had an excellent opportunity to compete nowadays. When you look at that team, and not just that team but other Celtics teams that also had a lot of balance, normally speaking we had at least 10 guys who could play."

Their chief asset was this "blood-thirsty" approach, Sanders said. The Russell Celtics simply wanted to win more than any team that has ever played the game and would let nothing get in their way.

As an example, Sanders cited the Willis Reed's heroic return despite a torn thigh muscle to help the New York Knicks beat the Lakers in Game 7 of the 1970 NBA Finals.

"When Willis Reed came back into the game he could hardly walk in that series," Sanders said. "What you saw was that Wilt (Chamberlain) had a lot of respect for Willis, and you saw Wilt walking beside him showing concern during the game. With the Celtics, that never would have occurred. Russell would have taken off at every opportunity for the long pass. He would have taken advantage of a player, in this case Willis, who was hurt. Red (Auerbach) pushed that very hard. And those things gave you points."

"We would play all these teams and we would zero in on their weaknesses," Heinsohn said in agreement.

Abdul-Jabbar always believed that Auerbach, Boston's great coach and general manager, always stoked the fire. "Red would do anything to win," Kareem once observed. "Anything."

Auerbach built a deep, deep roster for Russell to lead, and both coach and star player drove them with this blood-thirsty approach.

"We're talking about having advantages on other teams that wouldn't have had that approach," Sanders explained.

Likewise, no one could accuse Michael Jordan of not being blood-thirsty enough. Coach Phil Jackson may have motivated his players with his psychological approach, but Jordan burnished his teammates with his fierceness.

That, and Jordan's tremendous ability, were enough to gain six titles.

The NBA is clearly the domain of people with marvelous athletic skills. It is such desire that separates the good from the great in both players and teams.

In that regard, the teams highlighted in this book selected themselves, by virtue of their accomplishments.

It's the reason the Lakers' "Showtime" team of 1984-85 ranks third on our list. Magic Johnson brought a similar fierceness although he dressed it up with a bright smile and a relentless Lakers running game.

Ditto for Larry Bird and the 1985-86 Celtics and all the other teams on this list. They all had that fire inside. In that regard, picking the teams for this book was easy. We simply took the ones that burned the brightest and longest.

— *Roland Lazenby*

1962-63 BOSTON CELTICS

Front row, left to right, K.C. Jones, Bill Russell, President Walter A. Brown, Coach Red Auerbach, Treasurer Lou Pieri, Capt. Bob Cousy, Sam Jones. Standing, Frank Ramsey, Ge Guarilia, Tom Sanders, Tom Heinsohn, Clyde Lovellette, John Havlicek, Jim Loscutoff, D Swartz and Trainer Buddy LeRoux.

(Photo Buckley

When Pat Riley coached the Los Angeles Lakers' famed "Showtime" teams, he conjured up an aphorism that summed up the essence of championship play in professional basketball: "No rebounds, no rings." The team that controls the boards has the best odds of claiming the title and the laurels of greatness that go with it.

It was a simple conclusion for Riley, who was part of a generation that had witnessed the dominance of the Boston Celtics throughout the 1960s. The Celtics had won 11 NBA championships in 13 seasons, including an unmatched eight consecutive titles.

We chose the 1962-63 Celtics as the greatest NBA team of all time because it resided in the heart of that run of eight straight title teams. The best teams usually feature the best talent, and the '63 Celtics rule there, too. Seven players, all of them great, averaged double figures, and it was that deep, deep bench that made them a model for team play and propelled Boston to 58 wins in the days when the league played only an 80-game schedule.

1962-63 Boston Celtics

Coach: Red Auerbach

No.	Player	Pos.	Ht.	Wt.
14	Bob Cousy	G	6-1	175
21	Jack Foley	F	6-3	170
20	Gene Guarilia	F	6-5	220
17	John Havlicek	F-G	6-5	203
15	Tom Heinsohn	F-C	6-7	218
25	K.C. Jones	G	6-1	200
24	Sam Jones	G-F	6-4	198
18	Jim Loscutoff	F	6-5	220
4	Clyde Lovellette	C-F	6-9	234
23	Frank Ramsey	F-G	6-3	190
6	Bill Russell	C	6-9	215
16	Tom Sanders	F	6-6	210
12	Dan Swartz	F	6-4	215

Team Stats

PTS	PPG	REB	RPG	AST	APG
9,504	118.8	5,818	72.7	1,960	24.5

Regular Season
58-22; First Place – Eastern Division

Playoffs
Eastern Division Finals: Beat Cincinnati 4-3
NBA Finals: Beat Los Angeles Lakers 4-2

(Preceding page) The 1962-63 Boston Celtics. (Top left) Guard Bob Cousy got one more title for the Celtics in 1963. (Bottom left) Coach Red Auerbach smoked plenty of victory cigars, including the one for the 1963 NBA title, the fifth in the franchise's run of eight straight from 1959-66.

The Celtics' brash and brilliant coach and general manager, Arnold "Red" Auerbach, was an immensely competitive and polarizing figure in the game, but he also knew how to recruit and manage talent. "When you have a lot of stars, you have to keep them happy and playing as a team. Red did that," said former Lakers coach Fred Schaus. "I didn't like some of the things he did and said when I competed against him. Some of the things he said would bother me. But the guy who wore No. 6 out there bothered us more. You had to change your complete game because of him."

No. 6 was, of course, the legendary Bill Russell, whom Auerbach had drafted at a time when other coaches and general managers seemed to be more focused on a player's skin color than his abilities on the basketball court. And Russell's abilities were numerous. He was a force on the boards, snagging 1,843 rebounds during the 1962-63 season. He was such an effective defensive rebounder that he drove the Celtics' running game by snaring rebounds and whipping an outlet pass to Bob Cousy for a quick score. He averaged 4.5 assists per game and finished seventh overall in the league.

Plus, Russell's intimidating presence at center allowed his teammates to gamble on defense. If they made a mistake, Russell proved to be the kind of center who made opponents stop and think before they moved. He interrupted the sense of timing of the entire league.

"He was the ultimate team player," Cousy said of Russell. "Without him there would have been no dynasty, no Celtic mystique."

Around Russell, who averaged 16.8 points that season, Auerbach fit an array of spectacular players, including Cousy, Tom Heinsohn (18.9 points per game), Sam Jones (19.7), John Havlicek (14.3), Frank Ramsey (10.9), K.C. Jones and Tom "Satch" Sanders (10.8).

Cousy was in his last season, but the revolutionary point guard still averaged 13.2 points and 6.8 assists in the days of much tighter statistical rules for scorekeepers awarding dimes. Under modern guidelines, Cousy's assists would easily register in double figures. He was backed up by K.C. Jones, who remains perhaps the best ball-pressure guard in the history of the game.

(Left) Cousy retired after the 1962-63 season having been a part of six NBA titles with the Celtics. (Opposite page, bottom left) Center Bill Russell was the consummate competitor during the Celtics' dynasty.

Auerbach had drafted Havlicek out of Ohio State just the previous year, and watched him play in camp that summer. "I remember I was stunned," the Boston coach recalled. "All I could think of was, 'Oh. Have I got something here? Are they going to think I'm smart?'" Havlicek proved his coach's intelligence by playing in all 80 games and scoring 1,140 points.

"Our team was very diversified and very focused on winning," Heinsohn recalled. "With Cousy and Russell, their personalities demanded that they win, and we went out there and played to win."

And win they did. After claiming the Eastern Division, the '63 Celtics then faced Oscar Robertson and his new and improved Cincinnati Royals in a seven-game

PRESIDENT KENNEDY MEETS BOSTON CELTICS AT WHITE HOUSE

The world champion Boston Celtics were honored on January 31, 1963, when President John F. Kennedy received them at the White House. Left to right: John Havlicek, Trainer Buddy LeRoux, Clyde Lovellette, K.C. Jones, Capt. Bob Cousy, Coach Red Auerbach, Jim Loscutoff, President Kennedy, Sam Jones, Frank Ramsey, Heinsohn and Tom Sanders.

shakedown in the Eastern Finals. Russell's team survived a Game 7 shootout in Boston Garden with a 142-131 victory.

In the championship series, the Celtics took a 3-1 lead over the Lakers. Auerbach was as confident as ever. "We've never lost three games in a row," he told reporters.

Boston closed their fifth straight title out in Game 6 in LA. Havlicek had the hot hand, scoring 11 straight points to put Boston up by 14 at the half. At 2:48 to go in the game, the Celtics were holding on to a 104-102 lead. Then Heinsohn stole a West pass, drove and scored. From there, Cousy worked the clock as he had in the old days. He dribbled out the last seconds of his career and threw the ball high into the rafters. Then he and Auerbach hugged as the final touch on a 112-109 win.

Cousy's career ended, and yet the Celtics stayed strong because his retirement opened the door for Sam Jones and K.C. Jones, and the titles kept coming for the Celtics and Russell.

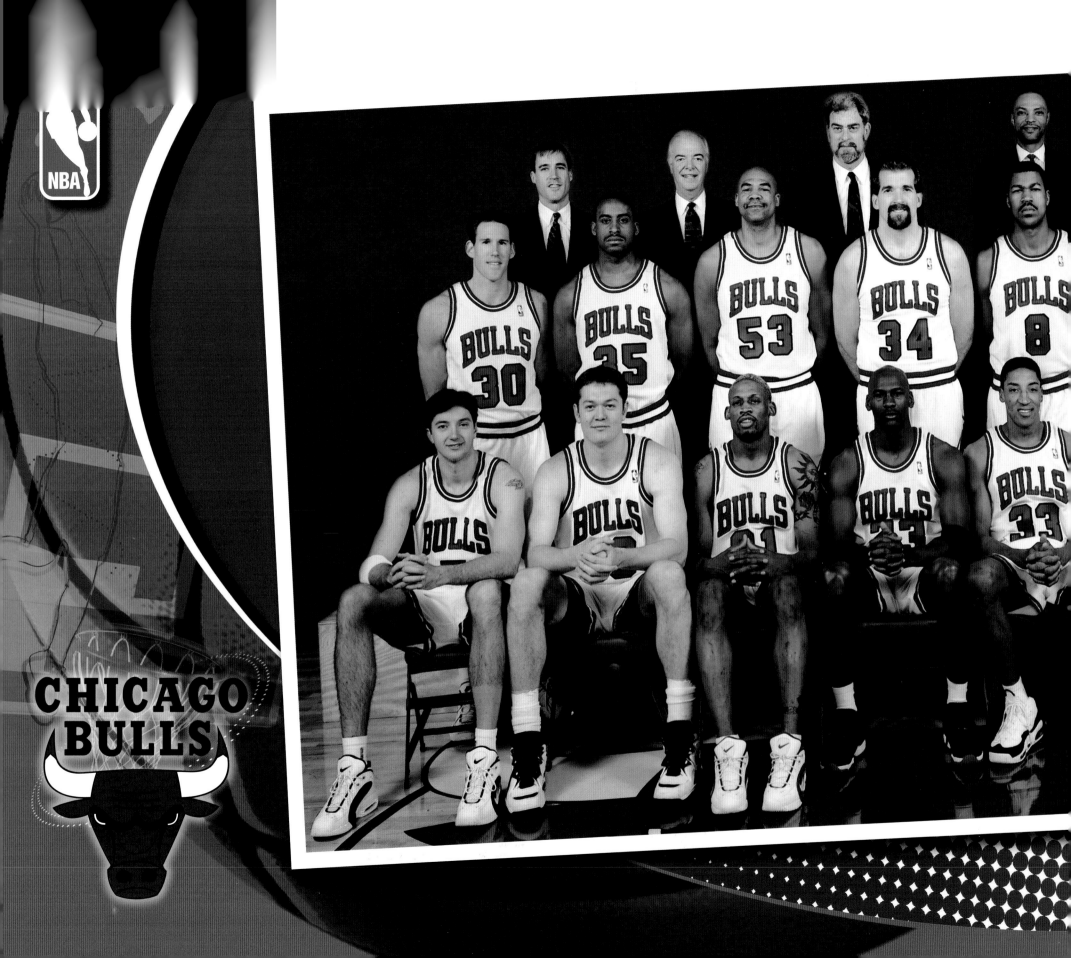

1995-96
CHICAGO BULLS

Jerry West once pointed out there are only about a half-dozen true superstars in the NBA at any given time. This was just as true when the league consisted of only eight teams in the early 1960s as it is in the 21st century when the league ballooned to 30 clubs.

No matter how many teams operated, the sport featured only a handful of truly great players during any season, West said. "Truly great players are very rare in this league. They always have been."

The rarest of the rare possess an unbending will to win that translates into fierce drive and team leadership. Clearly, Bill Russell and Michael Jordan stand out as the prototypes for these ultimate competitors.

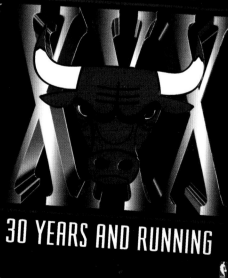

1995/96
MEDIA GUIDE

1966 CHICAGO BULLS 1996

30 YEARS AND RUNNING

1995-96 Chicago Bulls

Coach: Pat Riley

No.	Player	Pos.	Ht.	Wt.
0	Randy Brown	G	6-2	190
30	Jud Buechler	F-G	6-6	220
35	Jason Caffey	F	6-8	255
53	James Edwards	C-F	7-0	225
54	Jack Haley	C-F	6-10	240
9	Ron Harper	G-F	6-6	185
23	Michael Jordan	G-F	6-6	195
25	Steve Kerr	G	6-3	175
7	Toni Kukoc	F	6-10	192
13	Luc Longley	C	7-2	265
33	Scottie Pippen	F-G	6-8	210
91	Dennis Rodman	F	6-7	210
22	John Salley	F-C	6-11	230
8	Dickey Simpkins	F	6-9	248
34	Bill Wennington	C	7-0	245

Team Stats

PTS	PPG	REB	RPG	AST	APG
8,625	105.2	3,658	44.6	2,033	24.8

Regular Season
72-10; First Place – Central Division

Playoffs
Eastern Conference First Round:
　　Beat Miami Heat 3-0
Eastern Conference Semifinals:
　　Beat New York Knicks 4-1
Eastern Conference Finals:
　　Beat Orlando Magic 4-0
NBA Finals: Beat Seattle SuperSonics 4-2

(Preceding page, and left) The 1995-96 Chicago Bulls. Front row (from left): Toni Kukoc, Luc Longley, Dennis Rodman, Michael Jordan, Scottie Pippen, Ron Harper, Steve Kerr. Center row (from left): Jud Buechler, Jason Caffey, James Edwards, Bill Wennington, Dickey Simpkins, Jack Haley, Randy Brown. Back row (from left): John Paxson (assistant coach), Jimmy Rodgers (assistant coach), Phil Jackson (head coach), Jim Cleamons (assistant coach), Tex Winter (assistant coach).

West's observation about greatness is a factor whenever anyone attempts the difficult task of comparing teams from one era with another. NBA players from yesteryear often point out that talent was packed tightly onto those old team rosters. In 1963, for example, the entire NBA employed just 80 players.

Obviously, today's conventional wisdom is that weightlifting and other modern training methods have produced athletes who can jump higher, run faster and compete longer than those of yesteryear.

That argument certainly fits the 1995-96 Chicago Bulls who set the all-time mark for wins in a season with a 72-10 record. They reached that peak while winning six NBA championships in eight seasons. Jordan's attempt to play professional baseball in 1994 and part of 1995 brought the only gap in their run.

It was clearly the best-trained, hardest-working team in pro basketball history, with Jordan, Scottie Pippen and Dennis Rodman all pursuing a maniacal personal training regimen. And that was outside of practice. In practice, they embraced a zealotry unheard of in pro sports. Much of that effort was aimed at perfecting all the skills and drills necessary to run the triangle offense devised by legendary assistant coach Tex Winter.

The result was a disciplined style of offensive play that made it very difficult for opponents to double Jordan, arguably the greatest post weapon in the history of the game even though he was a guard/forward. The triangle offense allowed Jordan to work behind opposing defenses from the weak side, where he was a ruthless terror.

On defense, the Bulls used their size and athleticism to dismantle opponents like a gang of car thieves deconstructing an unattended Corvette. At 6-foot-6, guard Ron Harper was the amazing ball-pressure machine that wore down opponents. Rodman, at only 6-foot-7, brought another sort of versatility, using his tremendous strength to neutralize a great

center like the Orlando Magic's Shaquille O'Neal or turning on his quickness to snatch offensive rebounds in bunches.

At 6-foot-8, the long-armed Pippen had matured into a unique weapon, able to regulate the complicated triangle offense as cunning point forward. On defense, he covered the floor like a raptor, double teaming in the post, then recovering to the perimeter to snuff an open shooter.

When they needed more length, they turned to 7-foot-2 starting center Luc Longley, who possessed the size that coach Phil Jackson loved. Jackson explained in discussing Longley, "There are only so many dinosaurs," so many players with that rare, athletic size.

Perhaps the most confounding factor next to Jordan was Toni Kukoc, a 6-foot-10 point guard/post-up forward coming off the bench. The Bulls also had a 3-point terror in Steve Kerr and two backup centers who could score: Bill Wennington and James Edwards.

Unlike the 1962-63 Celtics, the 1995-96 Bulls featured only three players who averaged double figures in scoring: Jordan (30.4 points per game), Pippen (19.4) and Kukoc (13.1).

This assembly reaped all the rewards. The Bulls boasted the league's Most Valuable Player, the scoring champion (Jordan), the top rebounder (Rodman), the Sixth Man of the Year (Kukoc) and three members of the All-Defensive team (Jordan, Pippen and Rodman).

Beyond that, the club featured a deep, veteran roster that brimmed with size and smart players who knew where to find their shots in Winter's triangle. They were organized and coached by the tandem of Jackson and Winter, who would win 11 NBA titles in 19 seasons with the Bulls and Lakers. And they were motivated by their humiliating loss to the Magic in the 1995 playoffs just weeks after Jordan had returned from baseball that spring to resume his march through the NBA.

Fired by the sting of that defeat, the Bulls responded with a fury when the season opened in the fall of 1995. There to greet them was new teammate Rodman, a goofball with a Hall-of-Fame work ethic and a history of battling Chicago as a Detroit Pistons' "Bad Boy."

That chemistry propelled the Bulls to a 41-3 start to open the season, the best beginning in league history, better even than the 39-3 start of the 1971-72 Los Angeles Lakers, a club that tallied the best-ever single-season record at 69-13.

The sense of power was incredible, Pippen said at the time. "Nobody figured that an NBA team could have this type of pace that we're on right now. It's been a lot of fun really, almost like a college atmosphere."

Even Rodman, who was sporting crazily dyed hairdos that helped drive the Bulls' rockstar aura that season, acknowledged an unprecedented sense of power.

"I think a lot of teams are very afraid of the Chicago Bulls, just because of who the individuals are, just because they have to concentrate on so many people," he said. "A lot of teams are really skeptical. They're saying, 'What are we gonna do now? How are we going to play this team?'"

They rolled through the rest of the schedule, compiling a 39-2 home record and were 33-8 on the road.

As the playoffs neared, Harper donned a hat that said, "Don't Mean A Thing Without The Ring." Indeed, their gaudy record would

torment them if they didn't complete the deed with a title. Their focus was immaculate in the playoffs with a sweep of the Miami Heat in the first round. They dropped a game in New York on the way to beating a fine Knicks team 4-1. Then they humbled O'Neal and the Magic 4-0 in the Conference Finals, with Rodman simply moving the mammoth Shaq out of the lane like he tipped cows back in Oklahoma during his college days.

In the NBA Finals, the Bulls jumped out to a 3-0 lead against the Seattle SuperSonics. But Harper developed knee swelling before Game 4 and couldn't go. With the ball pressure gone from their defense, the Bulls lost two before Harper returned, and they claimed the title in Game 6 back in Chicago.

As Jerry West often said, greatness reveals itself. If so, the 1995-96 Bulls were nothing but a revelation.

(Preceding page) Jackson coached the Bulls to six NBA titles, but none more impressive than the 1996 championship after 72 regular-season victories. (Above) Jordan averaged 30.4 points in 1995-96 on the way to MVP and Finals MVP honors.

1984-85 LOS ANGELES LAKERS

Ask Los Angeles Lakers fans to pick their favorite "Showtime" team and they have a fine field to select from. After all, Magic Johnson led nine different teams to the NBA championship series during that era, and five of those clubs came away with the title.

Some fans have a fondness for the '87 Lakers. That was the year Johnson began to assert his offensive game after sharing those duties for years with center Kareem Abdul-Jabbar. Other Lakers fans think the best of those Showtime clubs was the '82 team, with Norm Nixon playing guard and Jamaal Wilkes manning the small forward slot.

Our selection, however, goes to the 1984-85 Lakers, coached by Pat Riley, who was in his fourth season at the helm and had emerged as the game's premier leader.

Abdul-Jabbar was still young enough to give the Lakers plenty. He was no longer

1984-85 Los Angeles Lakers

Coach: Pat Riley

No.	Player	Pos.	Ht.	Wt.
33	Kareem Abdul-Jabbar	C	7-2	225
21	Michael Cooper	G-F	6-5	170
32	Magic Johnson	G-F	6-8	215
1	Earl Jones	C	7-0	210
25	Mitch Kupchak	F-C	6-9	230
12	Ronnie Lester	G	6-2	175
11	Bob McAdoo	C-F	6-9	210
40	Mike McGee	G-F	6-5	190
43	Chuck Nevitt	C	7-5	217
31	Kurt Rambis	F	6-8	213
4	Byron Scott	G	6-3	195
35	Larry Spriggs	F	6-7	230
52	Jamaal Wilkes	F-G	6-6	190
42	James Worthy	F	6-9	225

Team Stats

PTS	PPG	REB	RPG	AST	APG
9,696	118.2	3,613	44.1	2,575	31.4

Regular Season
62-20; First Place – Pacific Division

Playoffs
Western Conference First Round:
Beat Phoenix Suns 3-0
Western Conference Semifinals:
Beat Portland Trail Blazers 4-1
Western Conference Finals:
Beat Denver Nuggets 4-1
NBA Finals: Beat Boston Celtics 4-2

(Preceding page, and left) The 1984-85 Los Angeles Lakers. Front row (from left): Dr. Jerry Buss (owner), Mike McGee, Kurt Rambis, Jamaal Wilkes, Kareem Abdul-Jabbar, Bob McAdoo, Magic Johnson, Michael Cooper, Bill Bertka (assistant coach). Back row (from left): Pat Riley (head coach), Byron Scott, Larry Spriggs, James Worthy, Mitch Kupchak, Ronnie Lester, Dave Wohl (assistant coach) and Gary Vitti (trainer).

dominant, but he still provided the Lakers a formidable half-court weapon when they needed it. Beyond that, James Worthy had quietly come into his own as a forward in his third season. He had brilliant quickness, and once Johnson got him the ball in the low post, the result was usually a score. He took delight in faking one way, then exploding another. And he continued to add range to his shot, building consistency from 15 feet out.

The Lakers again got good frontcourt minutes and scoring from former league MVP Bob McAdoo. In the backcourt, Michael Cooper had found his identity as a defensive and 3-point specialist, while third-year guard Mike McGee contributed 9.8 points per game.

Off guard Byron Scott had also matured nicely to provide excellent perimeter scoring. Handling the rebounding and heavy lifting were A.C. Green and Kurt Rambis.

It all added up to make the Lakers arguably the greatest running team in the history of the game, one that fed the break off its trapping defense.

"We were just pushing that ball up and down," Johnson recalled. "We didn't give you a chance to rest at any time in the game. We utilized everybody's talent. Kareem would get the rebound and say, 'OK, you guys just run on down the floor. Now if you don't score, you call me down and I'll come down and shoot the skyhook.' But first you go for option No.1 (which was Magic himself). Option No. 2, that's James Worthy. No. 3, probably Byron. No. 4, Kurt, A.C. or whoever is trailing. But we were gonna go through all those options before we said, 'Big fella, come down and save us right quick 'cause we couldn't score.' But we wanted to run at every opportunity. Made basket. Missed basket. Coach Riley had a saying, 'It may not have any effect in the first quarter. The running game may not have any effect in the second quarter, but by that third quarter and the end of that third quarter, it's going to have some effect.' And sure enough, we would usually take over that game by

the fourth quarter because you would be so tired. It was beautiful basketball."

The '85 Lakers were a well-built team, but the true reason they rank third best on our list had to do with history. Johnson finally developed the mental strength to help the Lakers throw off their legendary oppression by the Boston Celtics.

When the Lakers advanced to the championship series to face the Celtics the previous year, in 1984, Johnson and his teammates had heard about the Boston curse that had brought the Lakers seven title losses to the Celtics from 1959-69. That seemed like ancient history to Magic and his teammates until they lost the 1984 NBA Finals in seven games to Larry Bird and the Celtics.

It was a series Los Angeles had been favored to win. Suddenly the Showtime Lakers understood.

Riley and his players spent the 1984-85 season stoking their fires for a rematch. They knew they had to develop a different mindset, a real toughness to beat Boston.

"That first series that we gave them in '84 really seasoned us," Abdul-Jabbar recalled. "It gave us the mental tenacity that we didn't always exhibit. We couldn't outrun everybody. We had to understand that sometimes there were other ways to skin the cat."

As a group, the Lakers were driven by their '84 humiliation.

"Those wounds from last June stayed open all summer," Riley said as the playoffs neared. "Now the misery has subsided, but it never leaves your mind completely. Magic is very sensitive to what people think about him, and in his own mind I think he heard those questions over and over again to the point where he began to rationalize and say, 'Maybe I do have to concentrate more.' I think the whole experience has made him grow up in a lot of ways."

With a 63-19 regular-season finish, the Celtics had again claimed the home-court advantage. The Lakers had finished 62-20.

And neither team dallied in the playoffs. Boston dismissed Cleveland, Detroit and Philadelphia in quick succession. The Lakers rolled past Phoenix, Portland and Denver.

For the first time in years, the Finals returned to a 2-3-2 format, with the first two games in Boston, the middle three in Los Angeles, and the last two, if necessary, back in Boston. Game 1 opened in Boston on Memorial Day, Monday, May 27, with both teams cruising on five days' rest. The Lakers, however, quickly took on the appearance of guys who had just come off two weeks on the graveyard shift, paced by 38-year-old Abdul-Jabbar, who finished the day with 12 points and three rebounds. The famed Showtime running game slowed to a belly crawl as the Celtics ruled 148-114, an outcome that would be forever known as "The Memorial Day Massacre."

The next morning in the Lakers' film sessions, Kareem moved to the front row, where he sat up and paid attention. "That game was a blessing in disguise," Riley said later. "It strengthened the fiber of this team. Ever since then, Kareem had this look, this air, about him."

"That set the tone," Worthy recalled. "That game was the turning point in Laker history, I think. We came back strong, and Kareem led the way. Riley, too. He stepped forward. It was the turning point in his career, too. He took his coaching to another level. It brought the last development of his coaching technique. It was to utilize all aspects."

From their terrible start, the Lakers lashed back and took down Boston in six games. Best of all, the clinching victory came in the Boston Garden where so many LA teams had faltered in the past.

The Lakers had finally conquered those Garden Ghosts. "I'll always treasure that," Abdul-Jabbar said of the '85 title. "We finally shut up that Boston crowd."

(Preceding page) Riley coached the Lakers to their second NBA title in four years in 1985. (Right) Abdul-Jabbar uses his patented sky-hook against Boston's Robert Parish in Game 6 of the 1985 NBA Finals. Abdul-Jabbar scored 29 points, 18 in the second half, as Los Angeles defeated the Celtics 111-100, the Lakers' first Finals series victory over their rivals after eight previous failures. Abdul-Jabbar was named Finals MVP for his efforts.

REPRODUCTION

LOS ANGELES LAKERS 25th ANNIVERSARY 1984-1985

1985-86
BOSTON CELTICS

Boston Celtics fans are fond of calling their 1986 club the greatest team in NBA history. And their arguments hold plenty of merit.

Forward Larry Bird was completing a run of dominance — three straight years as the league's Most Valuable Player. In that time he led the Celtics to three straight appearances in the NBA championship series that netted titles No. 15 and 16 for the elite Boston franchise.

Joining Bird in a huge frontcourt were future Basketball Hall of Famers Kevin McHale and Robert Parish. Both men possessed excellent 8- to 10-foot shots. Parish's weapon of choice was an arching, rainbow jumper, a surprisingly graceful shot.

For McHale, the turnaround fadeaway became nearly unstoppable. Over his first

1985-86
Boston Celtics

Coach: K.C. Jones

No.	Player	Pos.	Ht.	Wt.
44	Danny Ainge	G-F	6-4	175
33	Larry Bird	F	6-9	220
34	Rick Carlisle	G	6-5	210
3	Dennis Johnson	G	6-4	185
50	Greg Kite	C	6-11	250
32	Kevin McHale	F-C	6-10	210
00	Robert Parish	C	7-0	230
12	Jerry Sichting	G	6-1	168
45	David Thirdkill	F-G	6-7	195
11	Sam Vincent	G	6-2	185
5	Bill Walton	C-F	6-11	210
8	Scott Wedman	F-G	6-7	215
35	Sly Williams	F-G	6-7	210

Team Stats

PTS	PPG	REB	RPG	AST	APG
9,359	114.1	3,807	46.4	2,387	29.1

Regular Season
67-15; First Place – Atlantic Division

Playoffs
Eastern Conference First Round:
    Beat Chicago Bulls 3-0
Eastern Conference Semifinals:
    Beat Atlanta Hawks 4-1
Eastern Conference Finals:
    Beat Milwaukee Bucks 4-0
NBA Finals: Beat Houston Rockets 4-2

(Preceding page, and left) The 1985-86 Boston Celtics. Front row (from left): Danny Ainge, Scott Wedman, Alan Cohen (vice chairman), Jan Volk (executive VP/general manager), Red Auerbach (president), K.C. Jones (head coach), Don Gaston (chairman of the board), Larry Bird, Dennis Johnson. Back row (from left): Wayne Lebeaux (equipment manager), Dr. Thomas Silva (team physician), Jimmy Rodgers (assistant coach), Sam Vincent, Rick Carlisle, Greg Kite, Robert Parish, Bill Walton, Kevin McHale, David Thirdkill, Jerry Sichting, Chris Ford (assistant coach), Ray Melchiorre (trainer).

five years in the league, his arms seemed to grow, at least in the minds of those playing against him. As the Celtics' sixth man, he became known as a shot-blocking irritant at one end of the floor and a half-court nightmare at the other.

"You can't have somebody guard me one-on-one when I get position," McHale once remarked. "I make two or three fakes and that guy is going to move. I'll either get a basket or get fouled, and that can hurt a team. You have to double team in that situation."

Over the years, Boston coach K.C. Jones repeatedly referred to Parish as "the backbone of the ball club." Jones often spoke appreciatively of watching Parish fill the lanes on the break, not getting the ball, yet continuing to run, playing his role, even as a decoy. "He does get overshadowed with Larry and Kevin," Jones said, "but he does get the job done and is so strong in the hard areas — rebounding, blocking shots, defense. He has done it all."

In their years of playing together, Bird and Parish victimized opponents on countless pick-and-roll plays. "The thing about Robert is if he sets a pick, he's always going to roll," Bird said. "He's got good hands, and if he's not all the way to the basket, then he can pull up and hit that 8- to 10-footer. Robert sets a thousand picks for me in a game. That's my reward to him, to give him the ball like that. He's so big, he has a potential 3-point play almost every time."

McHale and Parish teamed with Cedric Maxwell and Bird to

greatest passing center with the greatest passing forward in the game. The result was an exhibition of ball movement and team play that left the rest of the NBA in another class. In December, they lost a game to Portland in Boston Garden. It would be their only home loss of the year.

They roared out and converted doubters at every stop. "Right now, there's no doubt that Boston is a much better team," Magic Johnson said in February 1986 after the Celtics beat the Lakers in the Forum to extend their record to 41-9. On their way to a club-record 67-15 season, the Celtics claimed a winning record against every team in the league.

Few people foresaw this amazing turnaround, including Bird, who had contemplated sitting out the 1985-86 season because of back pain. But the acquisition of Walton and guard Jerry Sichting from Indiana had convinced him it would be wise to hang around and see how things turned out. His reward was the kind of season that only superstars can dream about. He averaged 25.8 points and nearly seven assists, two steals and 10 rebounds per game. He shot .423 from 3-point range and finished first in the league in free-throw percentage. For the second consecutive season, Bird broke the 2,000-point mark. And he finished the year with 10 triple doubles.

At the NBA All-Star Game in Dallas in February, Bird had 23 points, seven steals, eight rebounds and five assists. Then he won the long-range shootout, and afterward raised his arms in triumph, shouting "I'm the 3-point king!"

Later, midway through the NBA Finals, he picked up his third league MVP award. "I just felt there was no one in the league who could stop me if I was playing hard," Bird said. "What makes me tough to guard is that once I'm near the 3-point line, I can score from anywhere on the court. It's kind of hard to stop a guy who has unlimited range."

His personal confidence was at an all-time high, and it infused the team and coursed through the roster. McHale responded to his first year as a full-time starter by averaging 21.3 points. His .574 field-goal percentage was fifth best in the league. He blocked 134 shots during the regular season and another 43 during the playoffs. The former two-time Sixth Man of the Year Award winner was named to the All-Star team and to the NBA All-Defensive first team.

Walton, meanwhile, jumped into McHale's vacancy and claimed the Sixth Man Award. He played 80 regular-season games for the Celtics (a career high for Walton) and gave them 20 minutes per outing. He shot .562 from the floor and had 162 assists.

The team's other acquisition, Jerry Sichting, shot an amazing .570 from the floor as a backcourt sub.

And Parish averaged 9.5 rebounds and 16.1 points per game while shooting .549 from the floor. On occasion, he and Walton played side-by-side in a twin-towers setup. The towers became triplets at times when McHale joined them in the lineup. And if Jones didn't need size, he could go to a smaller, quicker group with Bird, Scott Wedman and McHale. The backcourt had similar depth with Danny Ainge, Dennis Johnson, Sichting, David Thirdkill and Rick Carlisle, all of whom contributed minutes, scoring and defense.

Boston swept Chicago in the first round, but not before Michael Jordan set the NBA abuzz with a 63-point performance in a double-overtime loss April 20 in Boston Garden. "That's God disguised as Michael Jordan," Bird said afterward.

From there, Boston rolled to the NBA Finals, where they again expected to find the Lakers, who had won 62 games. But Magic Johnson and company were shocked in the Western Conference Finals in five games by the Houston Rockets, who under former Boston coach Bill Fitch were employing a "twin towers" look with the 7-foot-4 Ralph Sampson and 7-foot Hakeem Olajuwon playing together.

They would match the Celtics' size in the NBA Finals but not their skill and experience.

Boston had the answer with Parish, Walton and McHale, complemented by double-teaming from Bird and Dennis Johnson. Although the Celtics received much praise for their unselfish crisp-passing offense, their defense helped bring down Houston.

"I don't remember the last time I was hounded by a team more than I was today," Sampson said after Boston closed out the series in Game 6. "Every time I touched the ball, there were two and three guys around me."

Playing at the top of his game, Bird averaged 24.0 points, 9.7 rebounds and 9.5 assists, and led the Celtics' double-teams of Olajuwon and Sampson as Boston took its place in history.

Bird was named the 1986 Finals MVP after he averaged 24 points, 9.7 rebounds and 9.5 assists in the six-game series against Houston.

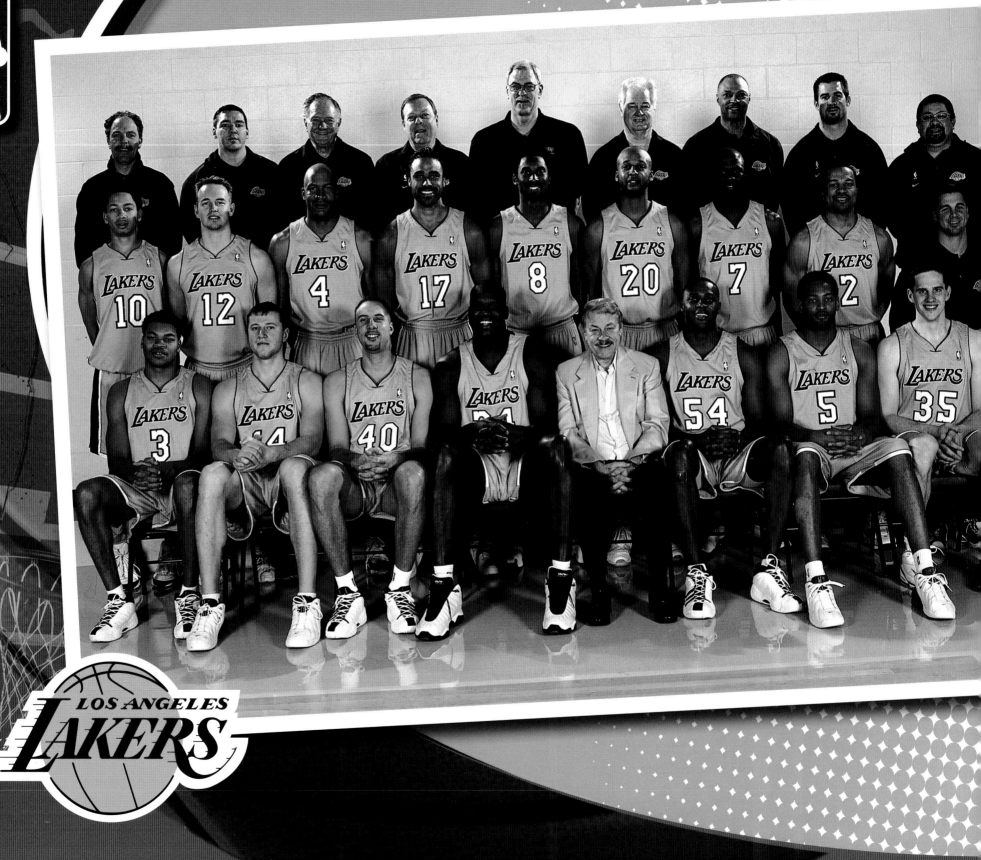

2000-01 LOS ANGELES LAKERS

After Phil Jackson departed the Chicago Bulls in 1998, he took a season off and then found a home in Los Angeles, where LA Lakers owner Jerry Buss had a very talented team with some serious issues. Center Shaquille O'Neal and wing Kobe Bryant possessed all the talent in the world but none of the chemistry needed to win a championship.

To change the culture of the organization, Jackson added Ron Harper, his master utility player from the Bulls. Harper settled nicely into the backcourt and would play a huge role in helping Bryant and O'Neal to work together, along with a host of fine role players, including Rick Fox, Robert Horry, Derek Fisher and Brian Shaw. This rebuilt team would go on to win three straight championships

2000-01 Los Angeles Lakers

Coach: Phil Jackson

No.	Player	Pos.	Ht.	Wt.
8	Kobe Bryant	G	6-6	200
2	Derek Fisher	G	6-1	200
40	Greg Foster	F-C	6-11	240
17	Rick Fox	F-G	6-7	230
3	Devean George	G-F	6-8	220
54	Horace Grant	F-C	6-10	215
4	Ron Harper	G-F	6-6	185
5	Robert Horry	F	6-9	220
10	Tyronn Lue	G	6-0	175
35	Mark Madsen	F	6-9	240
14	Stanislav Medvedenko	F	6-10	250
34	Shaquille O'Neal	C	7-1	325
12	Mike Penberthy	G	6-3	185
7	Isaiah Rider	G	6-5	215
20	Brian Shaw	G	6-6	190

Team Stats

PTS	PPG	REB	RPG	AST	APG
8,251	100.6	3,668	44.7	1,888	23.0

Regular Season

56-26; First Place – Pacific Division

Playoffs

Western Conference First Round:
    Beat Portland Trail Blazers 3-0
Western Conference Semifinals:
    Beat Sacramento Kings 4-0
Western Conference Finals:
    Beat San Antonio Spurs 4-0
NBA Finals: Beat Philadelphia 76ers 4-1

(Preceding page) The 2000-01 Los Angeles Lakers. Front row (from left): Devean George, Stanislav Medvedenko, Greg Foster, Shaquille O'Neal, Jerry Buss (owner), Horace Grant, Robert Horry, Mark Madsen. Center row (from left): Tyrone Lue, Mike Penberthy, Ron Harper, Rick Fox, Kobe Bryant, Brian Shaw, Isaiah Rider, Derek Fisher, Dan Garcia (massage therapist). Back row (from left): Gary Vitti (athletic trainer), Chip Schaefer (athletic performance coordinator), Bill Bertka (assistant coach), Frank Hamblen (assistant coach), Phil Jackson (head coach), Tex Winter (assistant coach), Jim Cleamons (assistant coach), Jim Cotta (strength and conditioning coach), Rudy Garciduenas (equipment manager). (Left) Bryant drives toward the basket against the 76ers in the 2001 NBA Finals.

between 2000 and 2002, the rare "three-peat," as well as making a fourth trip to the title round in 2004.

Although the 1999-2000 team was a 67-win juggernaut that stunned Jackson and his staff by winning the title that first season, we've chosen the 2000-2001 club as No. 5 on our list. Why? Because it sprinted through a 15-1 run in the playoffs, setting a record for dominance, after having to go on an 8-0 run just to finish the regular season with 56 wins.

At the beginning of the 2000-01 season, the Lakers seemed set to defend their title. That summer they had sent disgruntled scorer Glen Rice to New York while bringing in another stalwart from Jackson's teams in Chicago, Horace Grant, to fill the team's need at power forward. But things quickly unraveled. First, O'Neal had celebrated too hard during the offseason and came into training camp way out of shape, a development that deeply disappointed Jackson and his assistants, not to mention the hard-working Bryant.

Another key factor in the team's early struggles was the loss of point guard Fisher to foot surgery. He would miss three-fourths of the season before returning in March. As assistant Bill Bertka explained, Fisher was the only Lakers guard who could provide pressure on the opponent's ball handler.

Without ball pressure, the Lakers defense, so effective the previous season, now shriveled. The lack of defensive intensity only worsened the chemistry problems. O'Neal's lack of conditioning left him vulnerable to injury and poor play. With the center struggling, Bryant reasoned that he should take over the offense. In late December, Bryant would hit 20 of 26 shots to score 45 points in a win at Houston after which Jackson compared him to Jordan, but O'Neal fumed that Bryant was trying to hog all the glory.

Jackson pointed out that Bryant, who was leading the league in scoring as the new year neared, was playing the best ball of his young career. Some observers began calling Bryant the game's best all-around player. "He's got a level of commitment to his game and to wanting to be the best that few guys have," said Phoenix Suns head coach Scott Skiles.

The Lakers entered the new year with a 23-11 record, but a January *ESPN The Magazine* cover story on Bryant again stirred the team's conflicts. The story infuriated O'Neal, who told reporters that Bryant's selfishness was the main reason the team wasn't playing well. Jackson likened the two of them to little children arguing in a sandbox. Not surprisingly, the Lakers dropped four of their next seven games. Their 15 losses equaled the entire amount for the previous season.

February and March brought injuries to O'Neal and then rumors that the center and Jackson both were trying to have Bryant traded.

THE NBA'S GREATEST TEAMS

O'NEAL
34

2001 NBA PLAYOFFS

FIRST ROUND

EASTERN CONFERENCE

PHILADELPHIA vs. INDIANA
(76ers win series, 3-1)
Sat. Apr 21 Ind. 79 at Phil. 78
Tue. Apr 24 Ind. 98 at Phil. 116
Sat. Apr 28 Phil. 92 at Ind. 97
Wed. May 2 Phil. 88 at Ind. 85

MILWAUKEE vs. ORLANDO
(Bucks win series, 3-1)
Sun. Apr 22 Orl. 90 at Milw. 103
Wed. Apr 25 Orl. 96 at Milw. 103
Sat. Apr 28 Milw. 116 at Orl. 121
Tue. May 1 Milw. 112 at Orl. 104

MIAMI vs. CHARLOTTE
(Hornets win series, 3-0)
Sat. Apr 21 Cha. 106 at Miami 80
Mon. Apr 23 Cha. 102 at Miami 76
Fri. Apr 27 Miami 79 at Cha. 94

NEW YORK vs. TORONTO
(Raptors win series, 3-2)
Sun. Apr 22 Tor. 85 at N.Y. 92
Thu. Apr 26 Tor. 94 at N.Y. 74
Sun. Apr 29 N.Y. 97 at Tor. 89
Wed. May 2 N.Y. 93 at Tor. 100
Fri. May 4 Tor. 93 at N.Y. 89

WESTERN CONFERENCE

SAN ANTONIO vs. MINNESOTA
(Spurs win series, 3-1)
Sat. Apr 21 Minn. 82 at S.A. 87
Mon. Apr 23 Minn. 69 at S.A. 86

CONFERENCE

EASTERN CONFERENCE

PHILADELPHIA vs. TORONTO
(76ers win series, 4-3)
Sun. May 6 Tor. 96 at Phil.
Wed. May 9 Tor. 92 at Phil.
Fri. May 11 Phil. 76 at Tor.
Sun. May 13 Phil. 84 at Tor.
Wed. May 16 Tor. 88 at Phil.
Fri. May 18 Phil. 89 at Tor.
Sun. May 20 Tor. 87 at Phil.

MILWAUKEE vs. CHARLOTTE
(Bucks win series, 4-3)
Sun. May 6 Cha. 92 at Milw.
Tue. May 8 Cha. 90 at Milw.
Thu. May 10 Milw. 92 at Cha.
Sun. May 13 Milw. 78 at Cha.
Tue. May 15 Cha. 94 at Milw.
Thu. May 17 Milw. 104 at Cha.
Sun. May 20 Milw. 95 at Cha.

CONFERENCE

EASTERN CONFERENCE

PHILADELPHIA vs. MILWAUKEE
(76ers win series, 4-3)
Tue. May 22 Milw. 85 at Phil.
Thu. May 24 Milw. 92 at Phil.
Sat. May 26 Phil. 74 at Mil.
Mon. May 28 Phil. 89 at Mil.
Wed. May 30 Milw. 88 at Phil.
Fri. June 1 Phil. 100 at Mil.
Sun. June 3 Milw. 91 at Ph.

NBA FINALS

L.A. LAKERS vs. PHILADELPHIA
Wed. June 6 Phil. at LAL

GAME NOTES

555 N. Nash Street   El Segundo, California   90245   310.426.6000   310.426.6105 fax   www.lakers.com

LOS ANGELES LAKERS VS. PHILADELPHIA 76ERS
Wednesday June 6, 2001
NBA Finals Game #1

Upcoming Games

6/8	vs.	Philadelphia
6/10	at	Philadelphia
6/13	at	Philadelphia
6/15	at	Philadelphia*
6/18	vs.	Philadelphia*
6/20	vs.	Philadelphia*

*If necessary

LOS ANGELES LAKERS (11-0) (0-0)

					POSTSEASON AVERAGES		
NO.	POS.	PLAYER	HT	WT	PPG	RPG	APG/BPG
17	F	Rick Fox	6-7	242	10.1	5.1	3.5
54	F	Horace Grant	6-10	255	6.4	6.2	1.5
34	C	Shaquille O'Neal (C)	7-1	325	29.3	15.3	1.91/b
8	G	Kobe Bryant	6-7	215	31.6	7.0	6.2
2	G	Derek Fisher	6-1	200	15.1	5.0	3.5

RESERVES

40	C	Greg Foster	6-11	250	0.0	1.0	0.0
3	G/F	Devean George	6-8	220	2.0	0.7	0.1
4	G	Ron Harper	6-6	216	0.0	1.0	0.3
5	F	Robert Horry	6-10	235	4.7	5.3	2.3
10	G	Tyronn Lue	6-0	175	1.1	0.6	0.3
35	F	Mark Madsen	6-9	240	0.5	0.8	0.4
20	G	Brian Shaw	6-6	200	4.7	3.5	2.6

HEAD COACH: Phil Jackson (North Dakota '67)
ASSISTANT COACHES:
Bill Bertka (Kent St. '51), Jim Cleamons (Ohio St. 71),
Frank Hamblen (Syracuse '69), Tex Winter (USC '47)
TRAINER: Gary Vitti (Southern Connecticut State '76, Utah '82)
ATHLETIC PERFORMANCE COORDINATOR:
Chip Schaefer (Utah '83, Loyola Marymount '90)
STRENGTH AND CONDITIONING COACH:
Jim Cotta (Springfield College '93)
INJURIES: Greg Foster (sprained right foot) - doubtful

Recent Results

LAKERS
5/27 vs. San Antonio
LAKERS 111, Spurs 82
5/25 vs. San Antonio
LAKERS 111, Spurs 72
5/21 at San Antonio
LAKERS 88

PHILADELPHIA 76ERS (11-7) (0-0)

					POSTSEASON AVERAGES		
NO.	POS.	PLAYER	HT	WT	PPG	RPG	APG/BPG
33	F	Jumaine Jones	6-8	218	6.5	4.1	0.9
40	F	Tyrone Hill	6-9	220	7.4	7.5	0.4
55	C	Dikembe Mutombo (C)	7-2	265	13.1	14.2	3.39/b
3	G	Allen Iverson	6-0	165	32.1	4.5	6.8
8	G	Aaron McKie	6-5	210	16.4		

RESERVES

For a time, it appeared to some Jackson observers that the coach might even have panicked as his team fell apart before his eyes.

It was during the stretch, with team anxiety at its highest, that Bryant sat out 10 games with an assortment of injuries. The team went 7-3 in his absence, capped by a sweep of a four-game road trip in early April.

Closing the season with an eight-game victory streak revived their confidence and sent them on to their great finish. Just what was it that made the Lakers change for the good? Perhaps former team executive Jerry West, who reportedly told O'Neal, "I played with two of the all-time greats, Wilt Chamberlain and Elgin Baylor. You don't think we had personal rivalries going on back then? You've got to stop being a baby. Put all this personal stuff aside and do what's important. Put the team's success first."

During the playoffs, the Lakers swept excellent teams — Portland, Sacramento, and San Antonio — in order.

"We're built on the fact that Kobe and Shaq are the best one-two combination in the game," Jackson said, "and the complementary players around them want to play as a team and want to figure in this."

In retrospect, the veteran role players — Fox, Harper, Fisher, Shaw and Horry — would weigh large as a factor in the team's ability to win three straight titles.

"One of the main reasons they won the titles was the surrounding cast," explained one of Jackson's assistants. "Harper was a leader on the floor, Horry was an intellectual leader, Fox stepped up and helped the team find its emotional level, and Shaw was a spiritual leader. Those guys should get a lot of the credit."

O'Neal had averaged 33.7 points over the final 11 games of the regular season, and when Bryant returned from injury, the guard showed that he was ready to build on the center's energy. After all, O'Neal was now in shape and playing defense as well as offense. The two stars began working together, Bryant as a playmaker who found the right situation for exploding in big offensive games.

His first big explosion was in Game 3 against Sacramento, a 103-81 Lakers win that saw him score a career playoff high of 36 points. The Kings were keying on O'Neal, who had scored 87 points in the first two games.

In Game 4, the Lakers' 11th consecutive win, Bryant set another career high with 48 points.

"His enthusiasm infuses this basketball club," Jackson said of Bryant. "That's a real important factor to remember, that he's got the energy, the drive, the moxie and also a feel, an uncanny instinctual feel, for this basketball game that's really showing."

Bryant's momentum surged again in Game 1 of the Western Conference Finals, a 104-90

Tex Winter

Lakers blowout of the Spurs in San Antonio. Hitting 19 of 35 shots, Bryant had another 45, to go with O'Neal's 28.

"You're my idol," O'Neal said to Kobe afterward.

Bryant got great support from Horry, who had stepped up his game during the playoffs. In the first round against the Trail Blazers, Horry hit a 3-pointer with 2.1 seconds left to end the series in Portland. And in the conference semifinals, Horry nailed a 3-pointer with 56 seconds left to push the lead to 7 points as the Lakers eliminated San Antonio.

It all helped carry the Lakers on an 11-0 run into the NBA Finals against Allen Iverson and the Philadelphia 76ers. There, on the grand stage, it would again be O'Neal's time to dominate.

First, though, the Sixers erased the Lakers' perfect slate with an overtime victory in Los Angeles in Game 1. Afterward, Jackson chided O'Neal for his lack of defensive intensity. The center would respond by flexing his dominance over the rest of the series as Los Angeles swept the next four.

The Lakers simply ran through the injured Sixers in four straight games as O'Neal played brilliantly, blocking shots on defense and using his strength to control the tempo on offense. The ball went to the center, and he pounded the Sixers with a string of 30-point performances, to end it, once again, in the delight of the championship party.

NO. 6

2002-03 SAN ANTONIO SPURS

I t was Shaquille O'Neal who first nicknamed Tim Duncan "the Big Fundamental." Obviously Duncan drew that honor for his array of drop-steps around the basket and the way he kissed his jumper off the glass.

Hall of Famer Tex Winter, who as a Los Angeles Lakers assistant coach spent years studying Duncan's game, never bought into the nickname.

"It's hard to explain this guy," Winter once observed about Duncan. "He'll go spells without doing much on the court. Shaq called him the Big Fundamental. I don't know if his fundamentals are really that great in some instances. So what? This guy is great. You can't explain it, but you

2002-03 San Antonio Spurs

Coach: Gregg Popovich

No.	Player	Pos.	Ht.	Wt.
34	Mengke Bateer	C	6-11	290
12	Bruce Bowen	F	6-7	185
23	Devin Brown	G	6-5	220
10	Speedy Claxton	G	5-11	166
21	Tim Duncan	F-C	6-11	248
35	Danny Ferry	F	6-10	230
20	Manu Ginobili	G	6-6	210
5	Anthony Goldwire	G	6-1	182
3	Stephen Jackson	F	6-8	218
25	Steve Kerr	G	6-3	175
9	Tony Parker	G	6-2	180
50	David Robinson	C	7-1	235
31	Malik Rose	F	6-7	250
8	Steve Smith	G	6-7	200
42	Kevin Willis	F-C	7-0	220

Team Stats

PTS	PPG	REB	RPG	AST	APG
7,856	95.8	3,495	42.6	1,636	20.0

Regular Season
60-22; First Place – Midwest Division

Playoffs
Western Conference First Round:
    Beat Phoenix Suns 4-2
Western Conference Semifinals:
    Beat Los Angeles Lakers 4-2
Western Conference Finals:
    Beat Dallas Mavericks 4-2
NBA Finals: Beat New Jersey Nets 4-2

(Preceding page, and left) The 2002-03 San Antonio Spurs. Front row (from left): Mike Brungardt (strength and conditioning coach), Will Sevening (head athletic trainer), Brett Brown (director of player development), Joe Prunty (NBA scout), Speedy Claxton, Manu Ginobili, Stephen Jackson, Tony Parker, Steve Kerr, P.J. Carlesimo (assistant coach), Mike Brown (assistant coach), Mike Budenholzer (assistant coach), R.C. Buford (general manager). Back row (from left): Lawrence Payne (senior VP), Russ Bookbinder (executive VP), Dr. Paul Saenz (team physician), Rick Pych (executive VP), Dr. David Schmidt (team physician), Peter Holt (chairman), Malik Rose, Danny Ferry, Kevin Willis, Tim Duncan, David Robinson, Mengke Bateer, Steve Smith, Bruce Bowen, Gregg Popovich (head coach), Clarence Rinehart (equipment manager), Joe Gutzwiller (assistant trainer), Chris White (assistant strength coach), Scott Peterson (assistant video coordinator), Jimmy Chang (interpreter), Kyle Cummins (video coordinator).

sure can see it. He has the perfect competitive demeanor. His best talent is he knows how to play and utilizes his teammates. He's unselfish with a capital 'U.' And he's one of the best leaders in all of team sports. As a consequence, he makes everyone on the floor with him better, which is what they said about Larry (Bird) and Magic (Johnson). He's in that rare class. And a really fine defender. Blocks and changes shots. Works hard on glass …"

All of that helps explain how Duncan led the San Antonio Spurs to NBA titles in 1999, 2003, 2005 and 2007, and made celebrations a regular event on the famed San Antonio River Walk.

The success of the teams coached by Gregg Popovich means that any one of the four could be included on this list. We've selected the 2003 NBA champions in large part due to the roster. This season includes Hall-of-Fame center David Robinson as well as 25-year-old rookie Manu Ginobili, who brought a wealth of top international experience to San Antonio. A year later, Ginobili would lead Argentina to the Olympic gold medal.

Point guard Tony Parker, a shoot-first kind of playmaker, was just in his second year of pro experience, but he had started as a rookie and was on his way to an outstanding NBA career.

The same was true for athletic small forward Stephen Jackson, who was just 24 and in his third NBA season. He averaged 11.8 points a game.

The stopper was Bruce Bowen, who had come to San Antonio in 2001-02 to provide amazing consistency: 82 games played each season, about 31 to 33 minutes per game, reliable 3-point shooting from either baseline and adhesive defense that left opponents complaining of dirty play. Bowen would go on make the All-Defensive first team or second team for seven straight seasons in San Antonio while racking up a major consecutive games played streak.

Beyond that, the rotation featured energetic and versatile Malik Rose as a frontcourt sub and Steve Kerr as a gunner off the bench. The rest of the deep roster showed experienced veterans like Steve Smith, Kevin Willis and Danny Ferry.

Clearly though, the aircraft carrier was Duncan, who drew routine praise as perhaps the greatest power forward in the history of the game. He was in the midst of a run that included eight straight All-NBA first-team selections, two regular-season MVPs, three Finals MVPs and 13 All-Defensive first-team or second-team selections.

For 2002-03, Duncan would average 23.3 points, 12.9 rebounds and 2.9 blocks. But his 3.9 assists per game indicated just how much of the offense Popovich ran through the power forward. His passing skills demanded it.

Parker, too, was a force, averaging 15.5 points and 5.3 assists that season with a breathtaking quickness that allowed him to break

(Preceding page) Duncan shoots from the paint over New Jersey's Rodney Rogers (54) and Dikembe Mutombo (55) during Game 6 of the 2003 NBA Finals at the SBC Center in San Antonio. (Below) Popovich makes a point to his team during the 2002-03 season.

down defenses off the dribble to manufacture shots for Duncan or anyone sharing the floor with him. Parker's rapid development at basketball's most demanding position was a credit to Popovich, called "Pop" by the players.

"I think coach Pop showed a lot of confidence in me, helped me a lot," offered Parker, a Frenchman, in explaining his adjustment to the American game. "My teammates made my job a lot easier. They were very friendly. That helps a lot. I've got great teammates, great leaders with Timmy (Duncan) and Dave (Robinson). The key for me was Pop, because if he didn't show confidence in me ... Who's gonna take a 19-year-old point guard? From Europe?"

"So I think the hardest thing for me was to get the respect of my teammates," Parker said. "How is David at 36 years old gonna listen to a 19-year-old? So I think Pop helped me a lot."

Popovich, long known as a demanding coach, made discipline part of his formula for success without players chafing at his approach. The Spurs lacked much of the drama or squabbling present in other highly talented rosters. From the team's excellent management to Duncan to the many veterans sitting on the bench, the Spurs showed a strong capacity to focus on winning championships.

This was even more remarkable considering their diversity. With Parker, Ginobili and Duncan (who hailed from the U.S. Virgin Islands), the club stepped up as the first great NBA team with a decidedly international flavor.

There was also no question that after watching the Lakers claim three straight NBA titles, the Spurs were eager to have what Ginobili brought — toughness and energy that allowed him to shake up a game's tempo with his sorties to the basket.

They finished first in the Midwest Division with a 60-22 record, then launched into the playoffs, where they took the measure of each opponent, then polished them each off 4-2 in four straight series on their way to the title.

San Antonio ditched Phoenix in the first round, and then stepped up to face a Los Angeles Lakers team that had drenched the Spurs' playoff aspirations for three straight seasons. Lakers fans will point out that the 2003 season brought the distraction of coach Phil Jackson having to miss a playoff game against the Spurs after his doctors discovered his immediate need for an angioplasty procedure, following months of unexplained fatigue.

Despite Jackson's return to the bench, the Spurs eliminated the Lakers in six games, closing out the deed at Staples Center. The loss terminated Jackson's record run of winning 25 consecutive playoff series in Chicago and Los Angeles. The Lakers themselves had won 13 straight series, from the first round against Sacramento in 2000 to the first round against Minnesota in 2003.

It says much about the Spurs that they climbed the mountain to remove Jackson's teams from their perch lording over the game.

The defeat left Kobe Bryant, his teammates and the famed Laker Girls in tears, but in San Antonio it produced unrestrained joy. From there, the Spurs eliminated an outstanding Dallas Mavericks team for the Western Conference title, then they took the full measure of Jason Kidd and the New Jersey Nets 4-2 in the NBA Finals.

Duncan may not have been absolutely fundamental to the liking of perfectionist Winter, but to just about everyone else in the NBA, he reigned supreme. In addition to his 24.7 points and 15.4 rebounds during the playoffs, Duncan had cut up opponents with his passing to rack up 5.3 assists per contest, one of the all-time truly great performances.

His Spurs teams would go on to claim titles in 2005 and 2007 to make them clearly one of the greatest groups of competitors pro basketball had ever produced.

(Right) Duncan shoots over Mutombo in Game 6 of the 2003 NBA Finals. The Spurs clinched the NBA title with a 88-77 victory.

1988-89 DETROIT PISTONS

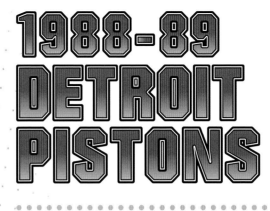

I n the late 1980s, after years of bottom feeding in the NBA, the Detroit Pistons morphed into a fearlessly physical defensive club with a dead-eye jump-shooting offense. For four straight years, they were as good as any team in basketball and routinely dismissed Michael Jordan and his Chicago Bulls. Coached by the legendary Chuck Daly, Detroit featured three tremendous guards, including the all-around great Joe Dumars and key reserve Vinnie Johnson, who Boston guard Danny Ainge nicknamed "the Microwave" because he heated up in a hurry.

It was the supremely competitive Isiah Thomas, though, who led the Pistons with a toughness born from his childhood in a Chicago ghetto. He was the little guy who never hesitated to rise up through

(Preceding page, and left) The 1988-89 Detroit Pistons. Front row (from left): Bill Laimbeer, John Long, Chuck Daly (head coach), Tom Wilson (CEO), William Davidson (owner), Jack McCloskey (general manager), Oscar Feldman (legal counsel), John Salley, James Edwards, Rick Mahorn. Back row (from left): Mike Abdenour (trainer), Stan Novak (scouting director), Will Robinson (assistant GM), Brendan Suhr (assistant coach), Micheal Williams, Vinnie Johnson, Fennis Dembo, Dennis Rodman, Mark Aguirre, Joe Dumars, Isiah Thomas, Brendan Malone (assistant coach), George Blaha (announcer).

1988-89 Detroit Pistons

Coach: Chuck Daly

No.	Player	Pos.	Ht.	Wt.
23	Mark Aguirre	F-G	6-6	232
45	Adrian Dantley	F-G	6-5	208
50	Darryl Dawkins	C	6-11	251
34	Fennis Dembo	F	6-5	215
4	Joe Dumars	G	6-3	190
53	James Edwards	C-F	7-0	225
35	Steve Harris	G	6-5	195
15	Vinnie Johnson	G	6-2	200
40	Bill Laimbeer	C	6-11	245
25	John Long	G-F	6-5	195
44	Rick Mahorn	C-F	6-10	240
12	Pace Mannion	G	6-7	190
10	Dennis Rodman	F	6-7	210
41	Jim Rowinski	F-C	6-8	250
22	John Salley	F-C	6-11	230
11	Isiah Thomas	G	6-1	180
24	Micheal Williams	G	6-2	175

Team Stats

PTS	PPG	REB	RPG	AST	APG
8,740	106.6	3,700	45.1	2,027	24.7

Regular Season
63-19; First Place – Central Division

Playoffs
Eastern Conference First Round:
   Beat Boston Celtics 3-0
Eastern Conference Semifinals:
   Beat Milwaukee Bucks 4-0
Eastern Conference Finals:
   Beat Chicago Bulls 4-2
NBA Finals: Beat Los Angeles Lakers 4-0

the trees to get to the rim. Later, Allen Iverson would mimic his moxieness, but "Zeke," as Thomas was known, was the NBA's original fearless little dude.

His attitude perfectly matched a frontcourt that featured the nasty work of Bill Laimbeer, Rick Mahorn, Dennis Rodman, James "Buddha" Edwards and John Salley. Laimbeer, Rodman and Mahorn led the intimidation that brought the Pistons their "Bad Boys" nickname. They were going to shove and grab and

hold, based on the idea that the officials couldn't call everything.

Mostly, though, they just wanted to win, and they would run through walls to prove it. They kept getting close, but they just couldn't establish that they were better than the Lakers or Celtics.

In 1987, they came achingly close to vanquishing Boston. With a 1-point lead and scant seconds to go in Game 5 of the Eastern Conference Finals, the Pistons were inbounding the ball under their own basket, and Thomas wanted the ball from referee Jess Kersey.

So the referee gave the Pistons guard the ball. He passed it in, Larry Bird stole it and hit streaking Celtics teammate Dennis Johnson for the go-ahead basket. Like that, Boston had a 1-point lead with a second left.

Boston survived and went on to the championship round.

The next season, the Pistons finally vanquished Boston, but had to face the mighty Los Angeles Lakers in the Finals. "We were the peasants, and they were the royal family at that time," Dumars recalls. Despite that, the Pistons held a 3-2 lead in the series when it returned to Los Angeles for the final two games. Yet once again, it was a case of being oh so close. Both of the final two games came down to the last seconds, and the Lakers won them both.

EMBRY: ARCHITECT OF CAVS' RISE

JANUARY 1990

NBA

hoop

FINALS MVP DUMARS LEARNS TO COPE WITH SPOTLIGHT

BEHIND THE SCENES: HOW DO COACHES DEAL WITH STRESS?

YOUNGSTERS TO WATCH: HORNETS' CHAPMAN, BULLETS' WILLIAMS

PLUS!

A COLOR POSTER OF SUPERSONICS' DALE ELLIS

$2.50

EDITION

WORLD NBA CHAMPIONS 88-89

PISTONS

DETROIT PISTONS

REPRODUCTION

(Left) Dumars was named MVP of the 1989 NBA Finals after the Pistons swept the Los Angeles Lakers in four games. He averaged 27.3 points and 6.0 assists per game in the series, including a 33-point effort in Game 2. (Opposite page) Thomas (11) dribbles the ball in the frontcourt against the Lakers' Orlando Woolridge (0) in Game 2 of the 1989 NBA Finals at the Palace of Auburn Hills.

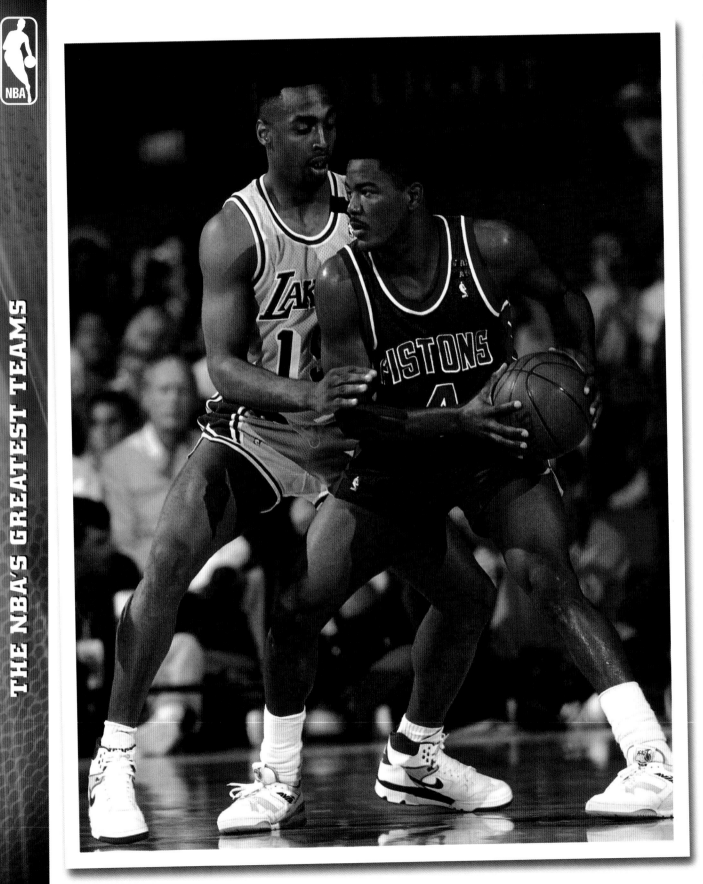

Having failed twice to bring home a championship, the Pistons made a major change in February 1989, when they traded Dumars' friend and mentor, Adrian Dantley, to the Dallas Mavericks for forward Mark Aguirre. Dantley was one of the game's premier scorers, but was notorious for holding the ball in the half-court offense. Aguirre was a better passer than people realized, and as a result, Dumars, known as a premier defender, became more involved in the offense.

Throughout the final third of the 1988-89 season, Dumars found himself taking more shots, and Daly noticed that the shooting guards for other teams had increasing trouble defending Dumars.

Dumars scored 42 against a strong Cleveland team in April, the game that clinched the Central Division title for the Pistons. In the third quarter alone, Dumars hit for a club-record 24 points. A team of many looks and weapons, the Pistons had suddenly found a new force to unleash, and Dumars' emergence that season as an offensive player took the team to the next level.

"I mean it was mindboggling," Daly said afterward. "I've never really seen him do that before, take over the game quite like that."

Thomas and Dumars became interchangeable. More and more during the stretch, Thomas would move to shooting guard and Dumars would run the point.

And Aguirre fit in perfectly at the small forward.

The Pistons finished 63-19 while showing a strong team concept. Six guys averaged double figures, but none of them above Thomas' 18.2 a game. Rodman averaged better than 9 points and nine boards off the bench. Dumars clocked in at 17.2 points per game followed by Aguirre at 15.5, Vinnie Johnson at 13.8 and the long-range shooter Laimbeer at 13.7 (he also posted 9.6 rebounds a game).

This unit promptly ran through the playoffs like a layup drill, as did the Lakers, led by Magic Johnson, who dismissed Portland, Seattle and Phoenix on an 11-0 run to the title series.

The Pistons easily pushed aside the Celtics 3-0 in the first round. The same fate befell the Milwaukee Bucks 4-0 in the second round. Only Jordan and the Bulls interrupted the trend. They won a pair of games from Detroit before falling 4-2. In retrospect, Dumars' physical defense on Jordan in that series (with help from Rodman and friends) remains one of the most unheralded performances in NBA history.

Left to wait while Detroit beat Chicago, Lakers coach Pat Riley worked his team hard. Some observers would later say he overworked them, when Johnson and Byron Scott were quickly felled by hamstring injuries during the championship series.

The basketball public expected a big clash. Instead, the Pistons swept LA during Kareem Abdul-Jabbar's final playoffs, and Dumars was named the MVP of the NBA Finals.

The Pistons had become even more guard-oriented during the playoffs as Thomas averaged 18.2 points, 8.3 assists and 4.3 rebounds per game while Dumars pumped in 17.6 points with 2.6 rebounds and 5.6 assists.

Afterward, Lakers executive Jerry West said privately that while the public perceived Thomas as the team's superstar, it was actually Dumars who deserved the distinction because he played so well on defense as well as offense. Dumars was quiet and gentlemanly, but he was every bit as much of a "Bad Boy" as the rest of his teammates. If folks doubted that, they only had to look to Jordan for confirmation.

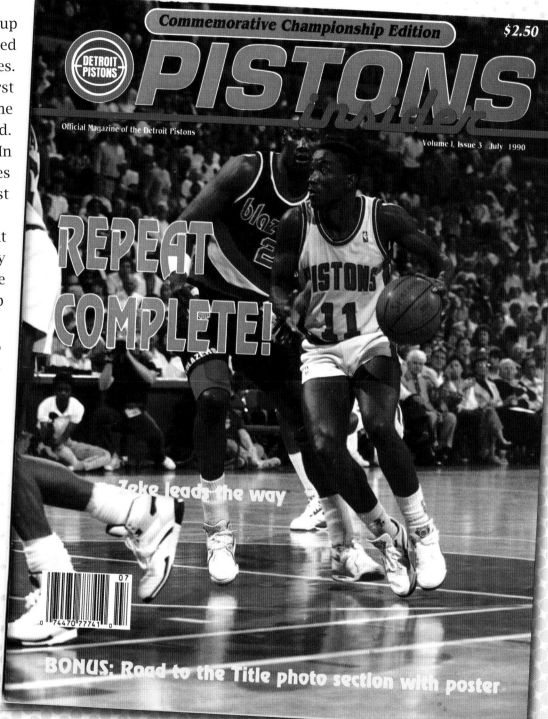

Commemorative Championship Edition $2.50

DETROIT PISTONS

PISTONS
insider

Official Magazine of the Detroit Pistons

Volume I, Issue 3   July 1990

REPEAT COMPLETE!

Zeke leads the way

0 74470 77741 0   07

BONUS: Road to the Title photo section with poster

(Preceding page) Dumars (4) looks to make a move around LA's Tony Campbell (19) in Game 3 of the 1989 NBA Finals in Los Angeles. (Right) Thomas, the firebrand of the Pistons' offense who averaged 21.3 points and 7.3 assists in the 1989 NBA Finals, would lead Detroit to a repeat title the following season.

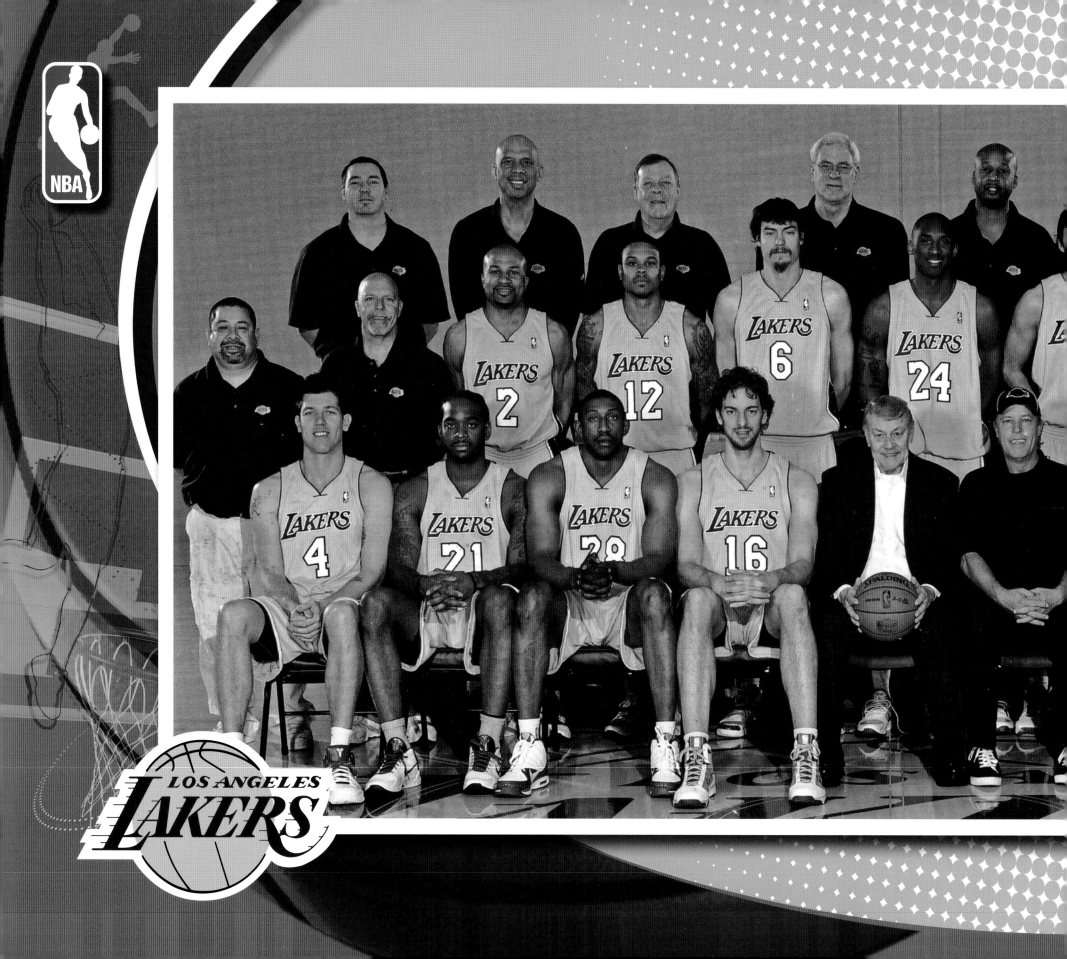

2009-10 LOS ANGELES LAKERS

2009-10 Los Angeles Lakers

Coach: Phil Jackson

No.	Player	Pos.	Ht.	Wt.
37	Ron Artest	F	6-6	244
12	Shannon Brown	G	6-4	205
24	Kobe Bryant	G	6-6	200
17	Andrew Bynum	C	7-0	285
1	Jordan Farmar	G	6-2	180
2	Derek Fisher	G	6-1	200
16	Pau Gasol	F-C	7-0	227
28	Didier Ilunga-Mbenga	C	7-0	245
6	Adam Morrison	F	6-8	205
7	Lamar Odom	F	6-10	220
21	Josh Powell	F	6-9	225
18	Sasha Vujacic	G	6-7	193
4	Luke Walton	F	6-8	235

Team Stats

PTS	PPG	REB	RPG	AST	APG
8,339	101.7	3,635	44.3	1,730	21.1

Regular Season
57-25; First Place – Pacific Division

Playoffs
Western Conference First Round:
    Beat Oklahoma City Thunder 4-2
Western Conference Semifinals:
    Beat Utah Jazz 4-0
Western Conference Finals:
    Beat Phoenix Suns 4-2
NBA Finals: Beat Boston Celtics 4-3

Hall of Fame coach Phil Jackson absolutely loved the opportunity late in his career to work with Pau Gasol, the 7-foot Spaniard known for his versatility and intellect.

The highlight footage ran from the routinely ridiculously good — Gasol in his face-up game, breaking down defenses — to the sublime — Gasol late in a blowout playoff win over Utah going behind his back on the dribble at midcourt to complete a sizzling assist.

Gasol's skills arguably made him the ultimate jewel of the triangle offense that Jackson employed to win 11 titles in 19 seasons of coaching, whether he was playing in the post, on the wing or in the pinch post (at the elbow of the lane).

(Preceding page, and left) The 2009-10 Los Angeles Lakers. Front row (from left): Luke Walton, Josh Powell, DJ Mbenga, Pau Gasol, Dr. Jerry Buss (owner), Jim Buss (VP/player personnel), Andrew Bynum, Lamar Odom, Ron Artest. Center row (from left): Rudy Garciduenas (equipment manager), Gary Vitti (athletic trainer), Derek Fisher, Shannon Brown, Adam Morrison, Kobe Bryant, Sasha Vujacic, Jordan Farmar, Marco Nunez (assistant athletic trainer), Marko Yrjovuori (massage therapist). Back row (from left): Chip Schaefer (director of athletic performance/player development), Kareem Abdul-Jabbar (special assistant coach), Frank Hamblen (assistant coach), Phil Jackson (head coach), Brian Shaw (assistant coach), Jim Cleamons (assistant coach), Craig Hodges (special assistant coach), Alex McKechnie (athletic performance coordinator).

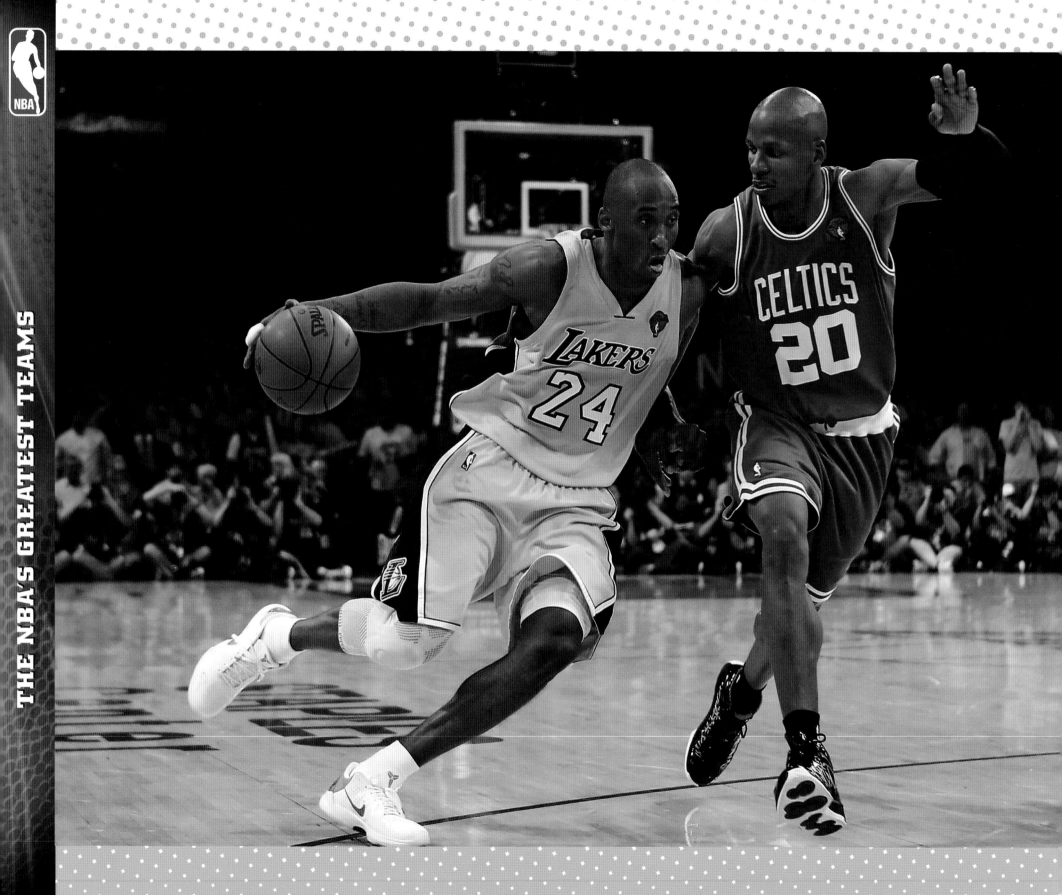

Gasol had a wicked face-up shot, and his spin moves in the post, right and left, brought to mind Boston legend Kevin McHale, except McHale never dreamed of Gasol's mobility. Or his court vision, for that matter. No-look passes and over-the-shoulder surprises dotted the Spaniard's resume.

Most important for Gasol was his timing. He came to Los Angeles with the Lakers struggling since last winning a title in 2002. Gone were Shaquille O'Neal and the cast from the "Three-Peat" era.

Only Kobe Bryant and Derek Fisher remained from those great teams earlier in the decade. The two guards shared a rock-ribbed competitive nature that made a perfect connection after Gasol arrived in Los Angeles after a February 2008 trade. His post play immediately helped Bryant and Fisher boost the Lakers to three straight trips to the NBA Finals.

In a little more than three years, Gasol took his rightful place among the pantheon of Lakers big men, right there in rare company with Kareem Abdul-Jabbar, George Mikan, Wilt Chamberlain and O'Neal.

At the same time, Gasol also managed to save the reputation of European basketball. There was a time that NBA insiders could hear the whispers around the league, complaints that European players were soft. In fact, after the Lakers were hammered by the Boston Celtics in the 2008 Finals, there was the quiet talk that there were too many Europeans on the roster.

During the series, Jackson said his players had had their "hearts cut out." Then the Lakers collapsed in Game 6 in Boston, giving the Celtics the series with a 131-92 victory. Surely it was the ugliest ending to a championship series in the league's history. Afterward, Bryant assured the media his teammates would find the mental toughness to come back from the devastation.

Sure enough, that next season Gasol stepped up his performance, with his rebounding, toughness and smarts.

There were other reasons the Lakers answered their own doubts in 2009 by winning 65 games and finding their confidence in the Western Conference playoffs. First they pushed Utah aside, then engaged the Houston Rockets and Ron Artest in a seven-game battle. From there it was a matter of disassembling the Orlando Magic 4-1 in the Finals, as Bryant was named Finals MVP.

Fisher confirmed that he was a key element, with clutch shooting of the same top order as former Laker Robert Horry. It was no accident that the Lakers' rise back to championship status had coincided with Fisher's return to the team after a three-year absence playing for Golden State and Utah.

The 2009 season also brought the maturity of center Andrew Bynum, who had to fight through injuries to help the team by the playoffs, and the emergence of forward Trevor Ariza, who likewise had been sidelined by injury and saw only a small piece of the 2008 playoffs. Ariza had responded to Jackson's coaching to become a solid 3-point shooter while deepening his knowledge of the Lakers' triangle offense.

And Bryant, the club's superstar, had finally become accepted as the hardest-working, best-prepared athlete in the league. Like Jordan before him, Bryant was not exactly loved by his teammates. But he had earned their immense respect.

The 2009 title also served to open the Lakers' eyes as to Gasol's stature. And it opened the door for one of the franchise's most satisfying championships, the 2010 victory over the Celtics.

The 2010 roster was decidedly different from the 2009 club in that Ariza was lost to Houston in the offseason and tough defensive forward Artest arrived as a free agent.

Where the 2009 club operated the triangle with high proficiency, Artest made the 2010 team much tougher defensively. Artest's struggles with the triangle offense meant that Jackson relied on the structured approach less and less. That and an assortment of injuries meant they won only 57 games in 2010, still good enough to win the Pacific Division.

The instability of the sudden roster changes had only heightened the team's appreciation of Gasol.

"Pau's always prepared," said Lakers' sixth man Lamar Odom that season. "You see him catch the ball and just go with that pretty left hook. He has an awesome array of moves and shots."

(Preceding page) Bryant (24) handles the ball under pressure from Boston's Ray Allen (20) in Game 7 of the 2010 NBA Finals at Staples Center. Bryant was named Finals MVP for the second straight season to go with the Lakers' repeat title.

The 7-footer missed the start of the 2010 season with a hamstring injury, but upon returning to the lineup and regaining some strength and flexibility, Gasol settled in to average 18.3 points and 11.3 rebounds, the perfect complement to Bryant's 27 points, 5.4 rebounds and 5.0 assists per game.

Bryant's big year highlighted the other measure of Gasol's impact — the double teams he drew virtually every time he caught the ball in the post.

"Teams double Pau a lot," Odom said. "A lot."

Those double teams created space for Bryant to move and attack. That was enough to earn top grades from that most demanding taskmaster of a teammate.

"My favorite player, to be honest with you, is Pau Gasol," Bryant told campers at his basketball academy. "His versatility is unmatched. He's a great example for a lot of kids. He can use his left hand as well as he can use his right. He's a big guy who can put the ball on the floor, post, shoot, rebound. He does everything fundamentally."

Gasol's alliance with Bryant resulted in an absolutely deadly screen-and-roll combo, one that kept the demanding Bryant smiling. It all added up to a perfect ending as the Lakers again advanced to the Finals and Bryant again claimed a Finals MVP award.

It was another major pelt in a career that would see Bryant pass his mentor, Jerry West, as the all-time leading scorer in Lakers franchise history. Bryant's feats included starting in every NBA All-Star Game since his second season in the league, a whopping 12 All-Star appearances, winning the All-Star MVP Award three times (2002, 2007 and 2009). He had been named 12 times to the All-NBA team and 10 times to the All-Defensive team. *The Sporting News* and TNT would name Bryant the NBA player of the 2000s decade.

As impressive as it was, none of it quite compared to Los Angeles beating Boston in a magnificent seven-game championship series in 2010.

Bryant had six assists and scored 30 for the 10th time in the previous 11 playoff games while Gasol secured 14 boards as Los Angeles whipped Boston 102-89 in Game 1 in Staples Center. In Game 2, however, the Celtics quickly wiped out LA's home-court advantage 103-94 behind Ray Allen's 11 3-pointers, a Finals record.

Tied at a game apiece, the series moved to Boston for Game 3 on June 8, where Bryant scored 29 while Bynum and Gasol had 10 rebounds each. The fourth belonged to Fisher, who scored 11 points on 5-of-7 shooting in the final quarter to finish with 16 in the 91-84 victory.

Boston then struck back to claim a 96-89 victory in Game 4 despite 33 from Bryant and 21 from Gasol. Working on that momentum, the Celtics overcame 38 by Bryant to take a 3-2 series lead with a 92-86 win in Game 5.

Could the Lakers win two at home to claim the title? They answered resoundingly with a 89-67 blowout in Game 6 back in Staples Center with Bryant scoring 26 and Gasol passing brilliantly out of the post for nine assists to go with his 13 rebounds.

The Boston collapse was driven by a first-quarter knee injury to center Kendrick Perkins. It all served to set up one of the franchise's most beautiful "ugly" outcomes in Game 7. Bryant struggled, and the Celtics surged to a 40-34 halftime lead. Gasol's rebounding (he would finish with 18), Fisher's heady play, Artest's defense and big shots all led to a Lakers revival in the fourth quarter that allowed them to tie the score at 64 with six minutes to go.

Tired and desperate, the Celtics began fouling as the Lakers inched to an 83-79 win that ignited delirium and cemented the 2010 Lakers' reputation as one of the greatest clubs of all time.

(Preceding page, top) Gasol's play at both ends of the court was a big reason why the Lakers were able to repeat as NBA champions in 2009-10. (Preceding page, middle) The Lakers' playoff media guide featured the franchise's eight previous NBA title trophies won in LA. (Right) Gasol grabs a rebound against the Celtics in the 2010 NBA Finals. (Inset) Jackson stands at the postgame interview podium after the Lakers won the title. It was Jackson's 11th title as a NBA head coach.

NEW YORK
KNICKS

1969-70 NEW YORK KNICKS

1969-70 New York Knicks

Coach: Red Holzman

No.	Player	Pos.	Ht.	Wt.
12	Dick Barnett	G-F	6-4	190
17	Nate Bowman	C	6-10	230
24	Bill Bradley	F-G	6-5	205
22	Dave DeBusschere	F-G	6-6	220
10	Walt Frazier	G	6-4	200
20	Bill Hosket	F-C	6-8	225
5	Don May	F	6-4	200
19	Willis Reed	C-F	6-9	235
6	Mike Riordan	G-F	6-4	200
33	Cazzie Russell	F-G	6-5	218
9	Dave Stallworth	F-C	6-7	200
16	John Warren	G-F	6-3	180

Team Stats

PTS	PPG	REB	RPG	AST	APG
9,427	115.0	4,006	48.9	2,135	26.0

Regular Season
60-22; First Place – Eastern Division

Playoffs
Eastern Conference Semifinals:
    Beat Baltimore Bullets 4-3
Eastern Conference Finals:
    Beat Milwaukee Bucks 4-1
NBA Finals: Beat Los Angeles Lakers 4-3

When Bill Russell retired after winning 11 titles in 13 years with the Boston Celtics, several teams aspired to the NBA throne. The 1970 New York Knicks and center Willis Reed claimed the prize by shoving aside Wilt Chamberlain and the Los Angeles Lakers in a mythical showdown.

In all, this New York team made three trips to the championship round in four years and won two titles. Starved for a championship, the city of media and style turned the celebration into a longtime affair. The Knicks easily set a record for books spawned by a championship basketball team.

Such musings aside, the 1969-70 New York Knicks were the epitome of "team" for that magical season. They didn't have one big star, just a bunch of guys with guts and a coach who taught them to believe in defense.

(Preceding page, and left) The 1969-70 New York Knicks. Front row (from left): John Warren, Don May, Walt Frazier, Ned Irish (president), Irving Mitchell Felt (chairman of the board), Ed Donovan (general manager), Dick Barnett, Mike Riordan, Cazzie Russell. Back row (from left): Red Holzman (head coach), Phil Jackson, Dave Stallworth, Dave DeBusschere, Willis Reed, Bill Hosket, Nate Bowman, Bill Bradley, Dick McGuire (chief scout), Dan Whelan (trainer).

The Knicks had sunk deeply into mediocrity through much of the 1960s, but that began to change in 1967-68 when they named scout Red Holzman to replace Dick McGuire as coach. Where McGuire had been nice, Holzman was tough and preached defense. "On offense, you guys can do what you want," he would jokingly tell his players. "But on defense, you do what I want."

Then, 29 games into the 1968-69 season, they traded center Walt Bellamy and guard Howard Komives to Detroit for forward Dave DeBusschere. It proved to be one of basketball's early lessons in "chemistry," a somewhat overworked term today. But back in 1970, the idea was relatively fresh. You take five good players, put them together, and find they aren't as successful as three good and two average players with chemistry. Coaches can rarely identify just what makes it work. They only know that it does.

Really, though, DeBusschere was a fine athlete. During the first four seasons of his NBA career, he also pitched in the Chicago White Sox organization. In 1964, just months after DeBusschere's 24th birthday, the Pistons named him as player/coach, the youngest ever in the NBA. Four seasons later he arrived in New York as a complete forward. Few people were better than the 6-foot-6 DeBusschere at the subtleties of rebounding, and he passed the ball as well as any frontcourt player in the game. Plus he had a smooth shot with great range and a superb basketball mind.

Holzman let DeBusschere install several key offensive plays that freed forward Bill Bradley to shoot, which in turn further opened up the offensive options.

The most important thing about the DeBusschere deal was the shifting of team roles that it brought. Komives' departure meant that third guard Walt "Clyde" Frazier moved in as a starter. Perhaps the best defensive guard in the league, the left-handed Frazier unmasked his offense once he got more playing time. His development as a scoring threat pushed the Knicks to the next level.

But most of all, the DeBusschere trade benefited Willis Reed, who had been playing out of position at power forward. With Bellamy gone, Reed moved to center, which set the team's identity.

"A lot of the pieces fell together at the right time," Reed said. Like Russell before him, Reed was quick and very intelligent. Unlike Russell, Reed had a smooth shot with plenty of range. Beyond all that, Reed had a presence that began with his physical power. He wasn't a great leaper, but he was strong and determined that no one would outhustle him.

"As a player and a man, he was always on fire," Frazier said of Reed. After five years in the NBA, Reed's hour had come around in 1969-70. First, he was named the MVP of the NBA All-Star Game, then later that spring, he was voted the league MVP. He capped that by picking up the MVP award in the Finals — the only player to capture all three in a single season at that time.

The Knicks had finished the 1968-69 season with a 54-28 record but lost to Boston in the Eastern Finals. "DeBusschere said in the locker room after the Boston series that next year was going to be our year," Reed recalled. "We really believed it."

After a great training camp, they opened the 1969-70 season by winning five, losing one, then taking the next 18, then a league record for consecutive wins. The Knicks rarely looked back from there, loping off to a league-best 60-22 finish.

In so doing, they transformed the Madison Square Garden crowd into a loud, silly horde. The upper deck screamed "dee-fense," and the city-hardened fans allowed themselves to believe. Like the Lakers, the Knicks also had their courtside celebrities. Woody Allen, Dustin Hoffman, Dianne Keaton, Elliot Gould

Sports Illustrated

MAY 18, 1970 60 CENTS

AFTER 24 YEARS
THE KNICKS
ON TOP

Dave DeBusschere fires
New York's final victory

(Left) DeBusschere was a *Sports Illustrated* cover subject after the Knicks won the 1970 NBA title in a thrilling seven-game showdown with the Los Angeles Lakers. (Opposite page, right) DeBusschere scores a layup against the Lakers in Game 1 of the NBA Finals in New York's Madison Square Garden. (Opposite page, left) Holzman moved from Knicks scout to head coach during the 1968-69 season and led the Knicks to their first NBA title.

and Peter Falk were regulars, along with comedian Soupy Sales and author William Goldman.

The Knicks had found their "chemistry," and it took them to the top. Another element was guard Dick Barnett, known as "Skull" because of his partially shaven head. He was known as a gun, but playing for Holzman required that he focus more of his considerable talent on defense.

Barnett also brought a looseness to the club. With Barnett and Frazier, the Knicks had the most stylish backcourt in the league. Frazier was "Clyde" from the movie "Bonnie and Clyde" because of his passion for a gangsterish hat and fancy suits. Barnett had the Carnaby Street look, complete with a cane, a cape and spats.

Cazzie Russell provided another huge scoring option coming off the bench behind Bill Bradley at small forward.

This amalgam clashed with Baltimore in the first round in a physical seven-game series. The Bullets had Earl "The Pearl" Monroe at guard, Gus Johnson at forward and Wes Unseld at center. The Knicks finally closed them out in the seventh game in the Garden 127-124.

In the Eastern Finals, they met Milwaukee with rookie Lew Alcindor (who later changed his name to Kareem Abdul-Jabbar), who had learned plenty in his first year. But the Knicks showed their veteran mindset and closed out the Bucks 4-1.

Then, in one of the greatest championship bouts in NBA history, New York stepped up to defeat the Lakers of Jerry West, Elgin Baylor and Wilt Chamberlain. Despite the Lakers' overwhelming edge in playoff experience, the Knicks were favored. Game 1 showed why. Although Reed had been worn down by battling first Unseld, then Alcindor and now Chamberlain, he quickly ran circles around Wilt for a 124-112 Knicks win. Reed finished with 37 points, 16 rebounds and five assists.

Chamberlain was much more active on defense as the Lakers claimed Game 2. Game 3 brought West's famous shot from 63 feet that tied the game at the end of regulation. But the Knicks won in overtime.

Game 4 brought another overtime, with Lakers reserve forward John Tresvant leading LA to a 121-115 win and a 2-2 series tie.

Wilt came out strong for the fifth game in New York and was determined to cover Reed all over the floor. The Lakers charged to a big lead, but the Knicks rushed back into in the second half after Reed tore a muscle in his thigh.

"I drove past Wilt and I just fell," Reed said. "I was having problems with my knee, and I tore a muscle in my right thigh."

A smaller lineup prompted a flurry of New York baskets to take a 3-2 edge in the series after a 107-100 victory. The Lakers returned home and corrected their mistakes in Game 6. With Reed out, Wilt scored 45 points with 27 rebounds. The Lakers rolled 135-113 to tie the series at three each.

The stage was set in New York for the seventh-game drama. Would Reed play? The Knicks left the locker room for warmups not knowing. Doctors had to place injections at various places and various depths across his thigh in an effort to numb the tear. Reed appeared on the Garden floor just before game time Friday, May 8, bringing an overwhelming roar from the crowd. The Knicks watched him hobble out, and each of them soaked in the emotion from the noise. The Lakers watched, too, and made no attempt at furtive glances.

1969 - 1970 WORLD CHAMPIONS

NEW YORK KNICKS

1969-70 NEW YORK KNICKS, FRONT: WARREN, MAY, FRAZIER, IRISH, FELT, DONOVAN, BARNETT, RIORDAN, RUSSELL
BACK: HOLZMAN, JACKSON, STALLWORTH, DeBUSSCHERE, REED, HOSKET, BOWMAN, BRADLEY, McGUIRE, WHELAN

REPRODUCTION

Once play began, Reed scored New York's first points, a semi-jumper from the key, and immediately Los Angeles sought to take advantage of his lack of mobility. Seventeen times the Lakers jammed the ball into Chamberlain in the post; Reed harassed him into shooting 2-for-9. Reed himself would finish 2-for-5 with four fouls and three rebounds, but it was enough. The emotional charge sent the rest of the Knicks zipping through their paces. They simply ran away from the Lakers. New York led 9-2, then 15-6, then 30-17. When Reed left the game in the third quarter, New York led 61-37. From there they rolled 113-99 to the title.

"It was a warm, wonderful time," DeBusschere recalled years later. Magical even.

(Preceding page, left) Reed tries to go around Lakers center Wilt Chamberlain during Game 7 of the 1970 NBA Finals. An injury in Game 5 knocked Reed out for the next game, but the Knicks captain heroically returned for Game 7 in New York. (Preceding page, inset) ABC's Howard Cosell interviews Reed and Holzman in the Knicks' locker room after the Game 7 victory over LA. (Top right) The 1969-70 Knicks team photo.

1971-72 LOS ANGELES LAKERS

The Los Angeles Lakers had lost seven times in the NBA championship series, six of them to Bill Russell and the Boston Celtics before dropping a seventh to the New York Knicks in 1970.

Soon they realized they were facing a new opponent with their veteran team — time.

That became even clearer when Elgin Baylor, at age 37, abruptly retired nine games into the 1971-72 season and was replaced at small forward by Jim McMillian. Lakers center Wilt Chamberlain had turned 35, and guard Jerry West was 33. The answer, in mind of Lakers owner Jack Kent Cooke, was to try yet another coach.

This time it worked.

1971-72 Los Angeles Lakers

Coach: Bill Sharman

No.	Player	Pos.	Ht.	Wt.
22	Elgin Baylor	F	6-5	225
13	Wilt Chamberlain	C	7-1	275
11	Jim Cleamons	G	6-3	185
14	Leroy Ellis	C-F	6-10	210
24	Keith Erickson	F-G	6-5	195
25	Gail Goodrich	G	6-1	170
52	Happy Hairston	F	6-7	225
5	Jim McMillian	F	6-5	215
12	Pat Riley	G-F	6-4	205
21	Flynn Robinson	G	6-1	185
31	John Trapp	F	6-7	210
44	Jerry West	G	6-2	175

Team Stats

PTS	PPG	REB	RPG	AST	APG
9,920	121.0	4,628	56.4	2,232	27.2

Regular Season
69-13; First Place – Pacific Division

Playoffs
Western Conference Semifinals:
 Beat Chicago Bulls 4-0
Western Conference Finals:
 Beat Milwaukee Bucks 4-2
NBA Finals: Beat New York Knicks 4-1

(Preceding page, and left) The 1971-72 Los Angeles Lakers. Front row (from left): Jim McMillian, Jim Cleamons, Pat Riley, Wilt Chamberlain, Bill Sharman (head coach), LeRoy Ellis, Willie McCarter, Ernie Killum, Flynn Robinson. Back row (from left): K.C. Jones (assistant coach), Elgin Baylor, Keith Erickson, Gail Goodrich, Fred Hetzel, Roger Brown, Rick Roberson, Malkin Strong, Jerry West, Happy Hairston, Frank O'Neill (trainer).

Out went Joe Mullaney, in came 45-year-old Bill Sharman, the former Boston Celtic who had just coached the Utah Stars to the 1971 American Basketball Association championship. He was a strange mix of fight and quiet innovation, all in the same package. He was a Southern California boy, but he was also a Celtic, and the Lakers weren't quite sure what to make of him.

"It was difficult for us to relate to him in the beginning, because he was covered with Boston green," recalled Pat Riley, a Laker sub at the time. "But in time we came around. He was a low-key guy, but very competitive, very feisty."

It didn't help that Sharman gave the Lakers another dose of green when he added K.C. Jones as his assistant coach. But the two former Boston guards brought just the right mindset to Los Angeles.

Sharman's major change was actually subtle. He asked veteran forward Happy Hairston to concentrate on rebounding. A bulky 6-foot-7, 225-pounder, Hairston complied and became the first forward ever to pull down 1,000 rebounds while playing alongside Chamberlain.

Sharman asked Chamberlain to focus less on offense, to rebound and play defense. And he asked West, in the middle of his advancing years, to move from shooting guard to point guard.

West complied, and he and guard Gail Goodrich each averaged better than 25 points per game that season.

Those adjustments worked perfectly for the Lakers in 1971-72. They won more games than any team in NBA history to that point with a 69-13 record, which in turn gave them the best winning percentage ever, .841. They had the most-ever games in which they scored over 100 points, with 81, the most wins on the road, 31, and the most at home, 38.

Best of all, they had their 33-game win streak, which ran through Jan. 9, 1972, when they lost a road game 120-114 to Milwaukee. Bucks coach Larry Costello had scouted the Lakers'

33rd consecutive win, a road victory over Atlanta, and quickly devised a defense to cut off their fast break.

"We knew it had to end sometime," Sharman said after the loss. "It was one of our weakest games in quite a while, but I think we learned something from it. It's hard to learn when you win."

With each victory, the mounting streak had boosted their team confidence. "We had been so snake-bitten in the '60s, to never ever win, always getting beat by Boston," Riley said. "When we won 33 games in a row, it was incredible."

They headed into the playoffs with a solid idea of what they wanted to do. Goodrich, who started with West in the backcourt, had become their leading scorer at 25.9 points per game. West scored 25.8 and led the league in assists. Chamberlain still held down the NBA's top spot in field-goal percentage and rebounding, and he still couldn't shoot free throws. The Forum crowd cheered loudly when he made one, and even louder when he missed.

As the playoffs neared, the team sensed that old Laker luck hovering somewhere nearby. "We were waiting for something to happen, something bad to happen again," Riley said. "But it didn't."

They moved past Chicago in the first round to meet their big challenge in the Western Finals — the Bucks and Kareem Abdul-Jabbar. In Game 1 at the Forum, the Bucks took away the home-court advantage, 92-73, when Los Angeles scored only 8 points in the third period.

The Lakers did manage a 135-134 win in the second game, but they were obviously shaky. West had shot 10 for 30 from the field. "I know what I'm doing wrong," he said afterward. "I'm turning my hand too much. But I can't get it stopped. It's got to go away by itself." At least part of the problem was Oscar Robertson's excellent defense on West.

The Bucks shot 61 percent for Game 3 in Milwaukee but still lost, as the Lakers drove frequently, drawing fouls and getting to the line. The big key was Chamberlain's defense on Abdul-Jabbar. Wilt overplayed Kareem to stop his sky hook, forcing him instead into short jumpers and layups. At one point in the game, Chamberlain blocked five shots. In the critical fourth period, Wilt held Kareem scoreless for the last 11 minutes. Abdul-Jabbar still finished with 33, but Chamberlain had done the job. The Lakers won 108-105,

(Preceding page, left) Goodrich drives on New York's Dean Meminger in Game 5 of the 1972 NBA Finals in Madison Square Garden. (Preceding page, inset) Sharman coached the Lakers to a 69-13 regular-season record, which included a NBA-record 33-game winning streak. The 1972 title was the franchise's first in Los Angeles, and first since 1954 in Minneapolis.

NO. 10 • 1971-72 LOS ANGELES LAKERS

and regained the home-court advantage. Goodrich scored 30 and McMillian 27 to lead LA.

The Bucks lashed back in the fourth game, taking a 75-43 rebounding advantage and tying the series at two-all, with a 114-88 blowout. Abdul-Jabbar celebrated his 25th birthday with 31 points. The Lakers took the fifth game in a blowout at the Forum, 115-90, then vanquished the Bucks 104-100 in Milwaukee to take the series 4-2. Their opponent in the 1972 Finals would be the New York Knicks, who had beaten a resurgent Boston club 4-1 in the Eastern Finals.

The Knicks, however, were not the team of old. They had lost Nate Bowman, Donnie May, Bill Hoskett and John Warren in the 1970-71 expansion draft. Cazzie Russell had been traded away after the '71 season to get Jerry Lucas from the Warriors. And Mike Riordan and Dave Stallworth were shipped to Baltimore in exchange for Earl Monroe.

Willis Reed was out of action with his nagging leg injuries, and Dick Barnett was also out. Lucas, who had starred with John Havlicek and Larry Siegfried at Ohio State, filled in for Reed at center. Dean Meminger and Phil Jackson were the chief subs. Earl Monroe was still troubled by his knees but able to work as a third guard.

In Game 1 in the Forum, Lucas scored 26 points and Bradley hit 11 of 12 shots from the field as New York shot 53 percent as a team. With that pace, they won much too easily 114-92. Early in the second half, the Forum crowd began filing out dejectedly. It looked like another Los Angeles fold in the Finals.

But in Game 2, the Lakers evened the series with a 106-92 win. Luck had always been such a big factor for the Lakers. Each of the previous Finals, they were overcome with a sense that fortune had turned against them. But that all changed after Game 2 in 1972. That night, West lay awake wondering how he would act if they actually had a championship to celebrate. He wasn't a drinker or a whoop-it-up type. How would he act?

At Madison Square Garden for Game 3, the Lakers danced out to a 22-point lead and regained the home-court advantage with a 107-96 win. In the first quarter of Game 4, Chamberlain fell and sprained his wrist. Obviously in pain, he decided to stay in. It was a crucial decision. The game went to overtime, but at the end of regulation, the Los Angeles center picked up in his fifth foul. In 13 NBA seasons, he had never fouled out of a game, of which he was immensely proud. Immediately speculation started along press row that he would play soft in the overtime. Instead, he came out in a shot-blocking fury that propelled the Lakers to a 116-111 win. "The patient is critical and about to die," Knicks guard Walt Frazier said afterward.

At first it appeared that Chamberlain would be unable to play Game 5 at the Forum. But as tipoff neared, Chamberlain received a shot of an anti-inflammatory drug and took the floor. Almost singlehandedly he was the Knicks' demise. He scored 24 points and pulled down 29 rebounds as Los Angeles finally broke the jinx 114-100. The effort earned Chamberlain his second Finals MVP award. Afterward, the Lakers sipped champagne from wine glasses. There was no shaking and spewing. No riotous behavior. West even found it in him to offer a toast or two. He toasted Sharman and then Chamberlain. "As for Wilt," he said, "he was simply the guy who got us here."

For West, the finish was rife with irony. After years of losing, his emotions were nearly empty, and when the Lakers got it, the championship seemed anti-climatic. "I played terrible basketball in the Finals," he recalled. "And we won. And that didn't seem to be justice for me personally, because I had contributed so much

in other years when we lost. And now, when we won, I was just another piece of the machinery. It was particularly frustrating because I was playing so poorly that the team overcame me.

"Maybe," he said after a moment's thought, "that's what the team is all about."

(Preceding page) West (44) shoots over a pick set by Chamberlain (13) in Game 4 of the 1972 NBA Finals in New York. The two stars combined to take out the Knicks in five games in the championship series. (Right) Goodrich (25) and Chamberlain (13) were featured on national magazine covers in the wake of the Lakers' title run.

1982-83 PHILADELPHIA 76ERS

1982-83 Philadelphia 76ers

Coach: Billy Cunningham

No.	Player	Pos.	Ht.	Wt.
7	J.J. Anderson	F	6-8	195
10	Maurice Cheeks	G	6-1	180
25	Earl Cureton	F-C	6-9	210
14	Franklin Edwards	G	6-1	170
6	Julius Erving	F-G	6-6	200
8	Marc Iavaroni	F	6-8	210
45	Clemon Johnson	C-F	6-10	240
33	Reggie Johnson	F-C	6-9	205
24	Bobby Jones	F	6-9	210
2	Moses Malone	C-F	6-10	215
31	Mark McNamara	C-F	6-11	235
4	Clint Richardson	G	6-3	195
3	Russ Schoene	F-C	6-10	210
22	Andrew Toney	G	6-3	178

Team Stats

PTS	PPG	REB	RPG	AST	APG
9,191	112.1	3,930	47.9	2,016	24.6

Regular Season
65-17; First Place – Atlantic Division

Playoffs
Eastern Conference Semifinals:
    Beat New York Knicks 4-0
Eastern Conference Finals:
    Beat Milwaukee Bucks 4-1
NBA Finals: Beat Los Angeles Lakers 4-0

During his basketball life, Julius Winfield Erving came to enjoy a splendid array of nicknames. As a kid in the Long Island, New York, community of Roosevelt, he was known as "Jewel." Then, as he established his prowess on Roosevelt's playgrounds, the name shifted to "Little Hawk," because he had massive hands that allowed him to control the ball off the dribble in a manner reminiscent of Connie Hawkins, the original "Hawk."

Finally, of course, Erving came to be known as "Dr. J." The Doctor set his own style, operating on the court as no one ever had. His manner and ability had made him one of the highest-paid stars in the NBA. It had brought him fame and respect. It

(Preceding page, and left) The 1982-83 Philadelphia 76ers. Front row (from left): Maurice Cheeks, Bobby Jones, Earl Cureton, Julius Erving, Reggie Johnson, Clint Richardson, Franklin Edwards. Back row (from left): Al Domenico (trainer), Jack McMahon (director of player personnel), Matt Guokas (assistant coach), Billy Cunningham (head coach), Clemon Johnson, Mark McNamara, Moses Malone, Marc Iavaroni, Andrew Toney, Pat Williams (general manager), John Kilbourne (conditioning coach), Harold Katz (owner), John Nash (assistant general manager).

had even gotten him close to three NBA titles, having reached the championship series in 1977, 1980 and 1982.

But for Erving, close wasn't good enough. Nor was it for Harold Katz, the new owner of the Philadelphia 76ers.

During the 1982 offseason, Katz sent center Darryl Dawkins to the New Jersey Nets and acquired the scoring/rebounding machine Moses Malone from the Houston Rockets.

From the very start of the schedule, the 1983 season had a championship feel to it. "Everybody had a sense that this was our opportunity," recalled Sixers forward Bobby Jones, who won the league's first Sixth Man Award that season. "The motivation was there, and we were healthy, too. We got off to a good start, got some confidence and didn't get cocky. We kept that good work ethic. I think Moses really established a lot of that. Julius had always had it. But then a big guy comes in and does that, and it helps."

Raised an only child in the hard-core neighborhoods of Petersburg, Virginia, Malone had found a familiar escape in the playgrounds, only his efforts went far beyond the typical basketball hard-work stories. He would shoot alone long into the nights, by streetlight.

Dick Vitale, then a college coach, recalled seeing Malone as a high school star at a summer camp. While the other campers were off at lunch, Malone stayed in the gym practicing his offensive rebounding. Time after time, he would tip the ball up and go after it. Fascinated, Vitale watched this effort and finally went over and asked Malone why he was doing it. "Coach," he said, "you got to get the ball before you can shoot it."

That tremendous drive to improve his rebounding made him a sensational star at Petersburg High, and instead of going to college, the 6-foot-11 center decided to sign a pro contract with the ABA's Utah Stars right out of high school.

Critics contended that Malone wasn't mature enough for the rigors of pro basketball. But he had turned 20 the spring of his senior year in high school and was very much a man — especially on the offensive boards. "When you get an offensive rebound, you're right there to shoot it back up," Malone once explained.

He wasn't much of a leaper, but he had a technique of powering back from the baseline to create position for himself. Time after time, he would snatch the offensive rebound and draw the foul on the put-back. Then he was deadly from the line.

Katz knew his team needed just such power and dedication in the frontcourt. So the owner signed Malone to a multi-year contract worth millions.

Some observers questioned the move. Malone wasn't exactly considered selfish, but his style demanded that he get the ball in the halfcourt. And he wasn't very good about passing out of the numerous double teams that came his way.

Those same observers wondered about Moses teaming with Erving. In many ways they were opposites. Malone was far from communicative, while Erving was perhaps the most urbane, articulate athlete in the game. And while Doc could leave earth at the foul line and float to the basket for a jam, the 6-foot-10, 265-pound Malone sat like a tank trap underneath. Erving had often commented that his one concern about flying was looking for a place to land.

"Won't Malone clog the runways?" observers asked.

The answer, of course, was "Sometimes."

But Erving and Malone had one tremendous thing in common during the Sixers' 1982-83 season — each wanted a championship ring in the worst way.

Erving provided the team with high-brow leadership. On the other side was the blue-collar Malone, solid as a block of concrete. "His was silent leadership," said Jones. "He always had confidence, and so you always had confidence because he was always so dominant at his position. Even if things weren't going right for you, you always knew 'Well, we can depend on Moses. Because every night he's gonna get the rebounds. Every night he's gonna put it back in and get to the free throw line.' That was reassuring."

Actually, this confidence ran the course of the organization, Jones recalled. "The talent was there. There was a realization that the owner of the franchise had taken the extra steps to get players and to bring a team together. Then it was up to the players and the coaches to step back from what our individual talents were and to play as a team and help each other to win."

(Opposite page) Erving (6) elevates over four Lakers for a finger-roll layup during Game 2 of the 1983 NBA Finals in Philadelphia. "Dr. J" averaged 19.0 points, 8.5 rebounds and five assists in the four-game sweep of the Lakers.

Malone averaged 24.5 points that season, matched by Erving's 21.4. They had Maurice Cheeks at the point, and Andrew Toney (19.7 points) at the off guard, and Jones coming off the bench. Coach Billy Cunningham managed to mix and match his lineups to perfection.

The Sixers ripped through the regular-season schedule with a 65-17 record. When writers asked Malone how the Sixers would fare in the playoffs, he uttered his famous "Fo, fo and fo" prediction, meaning that Philly would sweep to the title in 12 straight games. It was quite a brassy comment, yet Jones said it didn't anger the rest of the team. "Again, it was that Malone confidence," Jones explained. "It was confidence that he had backed up before with his actions."

Sure enough, the Sixers swept the Knicks in the Eastern Conference Semifinals and then confronted the Milwaukee Bucks in the Conference Finals.

The Sixers took the first three, then stumbled in a 100-94 loss in the fourth game. They quickly corrected themselves 115-103 in the fifth game to move on to the NBA Finals for the third time in four years.

There they met a hobbling and wearied Lakers team that had finished the regular season 58-24. Los Angeles had lost flashy rookie forward James Worthy to a broken leg a week before the playoffs opened. Even without Worthy, the Lakers overcame Portland and San Antonio in the Western playoffs. But their injury troubles continued into the Finals as Bob McAdoo and Norm Nixon would miss part of the series. Undermanned, the Lakers fell in line with Philadelphia's other victims during a 4-0 sweep of the championship series. Los Angeles would lead each game at the half, yet each time the Sixers would power ahead.

1982-83 PHILADELPHIA 76ers

SEATED LEFT TO RIGHT: Maurice Cheeks, Bobby Jones, Earl Cureton, Julius Erving, Mitchell Anderson, Clint Richardson, Franklin Edwards. STANDING LEFT TO RIGHT: Al Domenico (Trainer), Harold Katz (President), Billy Cunningham (Head Coach), Russ Schoene, Moses Malone, Mark McNamara, Marc Iavaroni, Andrew Toney, Jack McMahon (Assistant Coach, Director of Player Personnel), Pat Williams (General Manager), John Nash (Assistant General Manager). Absent when photo was taken: Matt Guokas (Assistant Coach).

The Lakers battled furiously in Game 4, and even held a 106-104 lead late in the game. Philly called a timeout. Having been burned by comebacks in the past, Cunningham told his players to close out the series before anything got started.

"I'm taking over," Dr. J said in the huddle.

He then scored 7 late points, momentum enough to push the Sixers beyond reach as they won 115-108.

Erving had finally nailed down an NBA title to go with the two ABA rings he had gotten with the New Jersey Nets. He, more than anyone, knew that no one player's effort was enough to win an NBA title.

"Let's not make believe," Cunningham said. "The difference from last year was Moses."

To remedy years of disappointment, it was just what the Doctor ordered.

(Preceding page, left) Malone (2) shoots a jumper over the Lakers' Kareem Abdul-Jabbar (33) and Magic Johnson during the clinching Game 4 victory for the 76ers in the 1983 NBA Finals. Malone was named Finals MVP after averaging 25.8 points and 18 rebounds in the series. (Preceding page, right) The 39-year-old Cunningham, a Hall of Fame player during his era, coached the Sixers to the 1983 NBA title.

MPLS.

LAKERS

1951-52 MINNEAPOLIS LAKERS

Center George Mikan teamed with athletic forward Jim Pollard to lead the Minneapolis Lakers to six pro basketball championships in the decade after World War II. The Lakers claimed their first title in 1948 in pro basketball's old National League, and then Minneapolis moved over to the NBA and took five titles in six years.

Mikan, at 6-foot-10, was so dominant in the NBA's first decade that his presence forced a rule change — the widening of the lane.

"Mikan was quite awkward actually, but his advantage in the league's early years was a lane that was only 6 feet wide," recalled Hall of Famer Tex Winter. "He used to set up position in close and go to work on opponents that had no idea how to stop him."

1951-52 Minneapolis Lakers

Coach: John Kundla

No.	Player	Pos.	Ht.	Wt.
16	Bob Harrison	G	6-1	190
11	Lew Hitch	F-C	6-8	200
15-4	Joe Hutton	G	6-1	170
22	Slater Martin	G	5-10	170
99	George Mikan	C	6-10	245
19	Vern Mikkelsen	F-C	6-7	230
10	John Pilch	F	6-3	185
17	Jim Pollard	F-C	6-4	185
18	Pep Saul	G-F	6-2	185
12	Howie Schultz	C-F	6-6	200
20	Whitey Skoog	G	5-11	180

Team Stats

PTS	PPG	REB	RPG	AST	APG
5,648	85.6	3,543	53.7	1,389	21.0

Regular Season
40-26; Second Place – Western Division

Playoffs
Western Division Semifinals:
	Beat Indianapolis Olympians 2-0
Western Division Finals:
	Beat Rochester Royals 3-1
NBA Finals: Beat New York Knicks 4-3

(Preceding page, and left) The 1951-52 Minneapolis Lakers. From left: Slater Martin, Joe Hutton, Frank Saul, Bob Harrison, Jim Pollard, Howie Schultz, Vern Mikkelsen, Lew Hitch, George Mikan. Not pictured: head coach John Kundla, Whitey Skoog.

Winter said he had often mused over what center Shaquille O'Neal would do with a lane only 6 feet wide. "Each possession would be a point-blank situation," Winter reasoned.

Finally, before the 1951-52 season, the NBA widened the lane to 12 feet. It didn't matter. Mikan led the Lakers to three more championships after the change, the NBA's first three-peat.

It was the era before the shot clock, which meant the Lakers could set each game's pace to suit Mikan, pro basketball's first great giant, who wore glasses with quarter-inch lenses.

Mikan went to DePaul during World War II as a clumsy, unpolished prospect who seemingly blossomed overnight into the premier player in college basketball — the big-time gate attraction during World War II. Remarkably, he developed agility while growing from 6-foot-8 to 6-foot-10. By the 1944-45 season, Mikan's junior year, he and Oklahoma A&M's Bob Kurland had become prototypes for what future generations would come to know as a "force." But when Mikan entered college in 1942, most coaches had little regard for tall players. Basketball was still the domain of the little man. Considered too awkward for the game, the big guys were called "goons."

"George and I opened the door to the idea that the big man could play the game," Kurland recalled.

Mikan and DePaul won the 1945 National Invitation Tournament, in those days the college game's prized trophy, and he twice led the NCAA in scoring. He did so by practicing what would become known as "Mikan drills," 250 right-handed hooks each day, then 250 left-handed, all at point-blank range.

He later became a force in pro basketball and carried the Chicago American Gears to a National League title, then joined the Lakers during the 1947-48 season.

His impact was immediate. Mikan would get position down low, drop his inside foot back, and pivot toward the hoop. As he did, he would lead his motion with his inside elbow.

"If you let Mikan get position, it was over," recalled Mike Bloom, a premier defender in that era.

"Mikan was great with those elbows," recalled Paul Seymore of the Syracuse Nats. "He used to kill our centers. Used to knock 'em down, draw the foul, then help 'em up and pat 'em on the fanny."

The other dynamic facet to those great Lakers teams was Pollard, the original "Kangaroo Kid," who had led Stanford to an NCAA title as a freshman in 1942, then starred in the old AAU leagues out west after the war.

At 6-foot-6 (he would always list his official height at 6-foot-4), Pollard was a rare bird in 1940s basketball. He could run, jump, dunk, dribble and pass. He could even execute a reverse jam, though not with so much twist and style as modern dunkers. No one envisioned a midair slam dance in 1947. But he could play above the rim. Many of the players in that whites-only era were mechanical, one- and two-dimensional athletes. Not Pollard. He was a prototype for the future.

The fans called him "the Kangaroo Kid." Later, Billy Cunningham would earn the nickname, but Pollard was the original.

"We used to know when Pollard had been in the building, because the tops of the backboards would be clean where he raked them," recalled Bones McKinney. "Pollard was fast, too. You couldn't press him either. He was too good moving with the ball. He'd get by you in a cat lick."

Because of that, Pollard often would serve as the Lakers' primary ball handler.

"If Jim had played in the modern NBA, he would have been a big point guard, like a Magic Johnson," offered Hall of Famer John Kundla, who coached that Lakers team.

The team won two titles, then made major changes with the selection of two key players in the 1949 draft. They selected 6-foot-7 forward Vern Mikkelsen, a power player out of Minnesota's little Hamline College, and 5-foot-10 guard Slater "Dugie" Martin out of the University of Texas.

Before the 1950 season was over, the new rookies would help make the Lakers into a blueprint for modern teams. Building around the 245-pound Mikan, the dominant center, and Pollard, the quick, acrobatic small forward, the Lakers transformed Mikkelsen into the original "power" forward. Martin filled the role of ball handler, or what would come to be known as a "point guard." Another rookie, 6-foot-1 Bob Harrison, found a place in the lineup as the off guard, another prototype as one of basketball's first "big" guards.

"We were the first team to have those types of players filling the roles, and we became the model for all the modern teams that came after us," Pollard recalled.

Marty Blake, a former NBA general manager and the league's longtime director of scouting, saw every team and every player in the league's history. "The Lakers were a great team," Blake offered. "Mikan and Mikkelsen and Pollard and Martin — they could have played today. Mikkelsen would be making $2 million a year, for God sakes. These people today don't realize how good they were."

The Lakers were also the first fully athletic team capable of dunking at will, but the ethic of that era didn't allow for such overtly macho statements.

For the most part, Mikan and Pollard built a deadly pick-and-roll routine, which Kundla called the J&G (Jim and George) play. Needless to say, it was the coach's favorite because most opponents couldn't stop it. "It was a simple little play," Kundla recalled. "But it was very successful."

That, too, would become a staple of modern NBA offenses.

The Lakers ran it again and again on their way to glory. We could have selected any of their six title teams for this list, but we settled on 1951-52, because it was won with the wider lane. Mikan was more dominant in the earlier championships, but the wider lane made them a better team because it gave the slashing Pollard more room to drive.

Beyond that, it meant more shots for Pollard and Mikkelsen, both of whom averaged more than 15 points for the first time in their pro careers. Heading into his third season, Mikkelsen defined the idea of power at the forward position.

"Widening the lane opened the middle and allowed these marvelous one-on-one deals," Mikkelsen recalled. "It helped all of us."

(Opposite page) From left, Martin, Mikan and Pollard carry off Kundla on Mikan's shoulders after the Lakers won the 1952 NBA title in seven games over the New York Knicks. Kundla coached the Lakers to five NBA titles in Minneapolis.

With the lane widened, the Lakers needed better outside shooting, and traded for 6-foot-2 guard Pep Saul, a two-handed set-shooting artist who helped open up the floor.

Mikan had been knocked out of the 1951 playoffs by an ankle injury, the only year they didn't win the title during their stretch run. He returned to the game in the fall and found it much changed.

His scoring average plunged from 28.4 to 23.8 points per game, which allowed the Philadelphia Warriors' Paul Arizin, one of the game's early jump shooters, to move ahead of him in the scoring race at 25.4.

As was often the case, the Rochester Royals nosed Minneapolis aside in the 1952 regular season, this time by a single game. But the playoffs were different. Gassed by the addition of Saul's perimeter game, the Lakers pushed aside the Royals 3-1 in the Western Finals. Then Minneapolis met the New York Knicks for the NBA championship.

In a surprise, the young Knicks forced the Lakers to a seventh game. But in Game 7 in the Minneapolis Auditorium, the Lakers won 82-65, giving Mikan the fourth of his six Lakers titles.

1993-94 HOUSTON ROCKETS

Michael Jordan's sudden departure from the NBA in 1993 had left the field wide open for a variety of superstars whose teams had never won a title. Clyde Drexler in Portland, Charles Barkley in Phoenix, Karl Malone and John Stockton in Utah, and Patrick Ewing in New York all had hopes of leading their clubs to the 1994 championship.

Yet none, perhaps, was more eager or more prepared than Houston's Hakeem Olajuwon. For eight consecutive seasons, he had finished with at least 100 steals and 200 blocks, a string unmatched in NBA history. For his first nine seasons in the league, Olajuwon had averaged better than 11 rebounds per game. Only Wilt Chamberlain (14 seasons), Bill Russell (13), Elvin Hayes (12) and Bob Pettit (11) had longer streaks.

1993-94 Houston Rockets

Coach: Rudy Tomjanovich

No.	Player	Pos.	Ht.	Wt.
1	Scott Brooks	G	5-11	165
50	Matt Bullard	F	6-10	215
10	Sam Cassell	G	6-3	185
35	Earl Cureton	F-C	6-9	210
17	Mario Elie	G-F	6-5	210
7	Carl Herrera	F	6-9	215
25	Robert Horry	F	6-9	220
21	Chris Jent	F	6-7	220
11	Vernon Maxwell	G	6-4	180
34	Hakeem Olajuwon	C	7-0	255
3	Richard Petruska	C-F	6-10	260
42	Eric Riley	C	7-0	245
20	Larry Robinson	F-G	6-3	180
30	Kenny Smith	G	6-3	170
33	Otis Thorpe	F-C	6-9	225

Team Stats

PTS	PPG	REB	RPG	AST	APG
8,292	101.1	3,545	43.2	2,087	25.4

Regular Season
58-24; First Place – Midwest Division

Playoffs
Western Conference First Round:
    Beat Portland Trail Blazers 3-1
Western Conference Semifinals:
    Beat Phoenix Suns 4-3
Western Conference Finals:
    Beat Utah Jazz 4-1
NBA Finals: Beat New York Knicks 4-3

(Preceding page, and left) The 1993-94 Houston Rockets. Front row (from left): Carroll Dawson (assistant coach), Robert Horry, Kenny Smith, Otis Thorpe, Rudy Tomjanovich (head coach), Hakeem Olajuwon, Vernon Maxwell, Larry Smith (assistant coach), Bill Berry (assistant coach). Back row (from left): David Nordstrom (equipment manager), Joe Ash (scout), Robert Barr (strength coach), Sam Cassell, Carl Herrera, Matt Bullard, Eric Riley, Richard Petruska, Larry Robinson, Mario Elie, Scott Brooks, Jim Boylen (video coordinator), Ed Bernholz (film coordinator), Ray Melchiorre (trainer). Not pictured: Earl Cureton, Chris Jent.

"Now that Michael has left, Hakeem is the most complete player in the game — there's no doubt in my mind," observed Cleveland center Brad Daugherty during the 1993-94 season. "He's 31 years old, an age when you're considered to be on the downside of your career, but he's just exploded into the greatest player in the league."

Olajuwon's journey to the highest levels of the game had begun in Lagos, Nigeria, in 1978, when he first played basketball at age 15. He would find his way to the University of Houston, where he interned three seasons under coach Guy Lewis, a master at teaching post moves.

Then, in 1984, the Houston Rockets made him the top pick in the NBA Draft, two selections ahead of Jordan, despite the fact they already had a Rookie-of-the-Year center in Ralph Sampson. The Rockets' answer was to play them together as the "Twin Towers." Sampson and Olajuwon presented matchup problems for opponents around the league, led the Rockets to an upset of the Lakers in the 1986 playoffs and a spot against the Celtics in the NBA Finals. They lost in six games, a defeat Olajuwon considered the most painful of his career, but he figured he was part of a team that would rule the NBA.

Instead, things fell apart. Sampson's knees went bad, and the Rockets traded him. Coach Bill Fitch was eventually fired, and the Rockets' front office never could seem to find a supporting cast to play with Olajuwon. Season after season of promise passed with no dividends.

By the 1990s, Olajuwon had established himself as the best center in the game. But more trouble followed as Olajuwon sought a pay raise to bring his salary in line with the league's other superstars. He soon found himself in an ugly standoff with the front office.

Rockets assistant Rudy Tomjanovich was promoted to head coach for the 1992-93 season, but the center's war of words with the team escalated, with his telling the press the Rockets were run by fools.

Fortunately, the Rockets faced a 14-hour plane ride for a game in Tokyo. On the trip, Olajuwon and owner Charlie Thomas talked out their differences and agreed on a four-year, $25 million contract extension.

With peace established, Tomjanovich went to work convincing his center to pass out of the double and triple teams he faced. In Olajuwon's defense, passing hadn't always been his best option, considering the Rockets' poor perimeter game. But Tomjanovich remedied that by setting up an armada of 3-point specialists around Olajuwon.

"When the Rockets are hitting their 3s, you might as well pack it up and go home," explained Phoenix forward Charles Barkley, "because you can't double-team Hakeem."

Houston made a nice run in the 1993 playoffs. Then they opened the next season by winning 18 of 19 games, which established Olajuwon and his Rockets as the primary contenders. Alongside him in the frontcourt were power forward Otis Thorpe and a host of utility forwards including Robert Horry, Mario Elie, Carl Herrera and Matt Bullard. The backcourt consisted of starters Vernon Maxwell and Kenny Smith and rookie backup Sam Cassell.

Despite hitting some turbulence along the way after their big start, this group had managed to fight their way to a 58-24 finish, second in the league only to Seattle's 63 wins.

With Jordan out of the NBA, the national press suddenly turned its focus on Olajuwon, prompting *Houston Chronicle* columnist Fran Blinebury to observe that Hakeem was "the elephant who has been standing smack in the middle of the living room for the past 10 seasons and is just beginning to get noticed by the experts sitting on the sofa."

For the fourth time in his decade-old career, Olajuwon ranked among the top 10 in four statistical categories. He finished second in blocked shots (3.71); third in scoring (career-high 27.3 points per game); fourth in rebounding (11.9); and 10th in field-goal percentage (.528).

His season began to look even better when the Denver Nuggets upset Seattle in the first round of the playoffs. Houston's path to the championship, however, was by no means clear. The Rockets promptly lost their first two second-round home games to Phoenix.

(Opposite page) Two of the NBA's great centers of the 1990s battled in the 1994 NBA Finals, the Rockets' Olajuwon (34) and the New York Knicks' Patrick Ewing (33). Olajuwon helped hold Ewing to 36.4 percent shooting from the floor as the Rockets won the title in seven games.

Olajuwon told reporters that you can't tell about the character of a team when it's winning. You have to wait until times get tough. At the time, only one other team in NBA history, the 1969 Lakers, had come back after losing its first two games at home in a seven-game series. But with Olajuwon ruling the lane the Rockets caught the Suns and escaped with a Game 7 victory in Houston. From there, they nixed Utah 4-1 in the Western Finals and came face-to-face with Patrick Ewing and the Knicks, who had survived a seven-game series with the Jordan-less Bulls.

A decade earlier, Ewing's Georgetown Hoyas had defeated Olajuwon's Houston Cougars for the 1984 NCAA title. The NBA rematch would be a seven-game showdown for the league title, with the Rockets holding home-court advantage.

Each night during warmups, with a jazz band blaring nearby, Olajuwon would choreograph his spinning post moves. Like a dancer, he would whirl with the ball cradled in his arm, pivoting first right, then left. He'd pause, facing the goal, to execute a jab step. Up and back. Leaning in with the ball pulled into his waist, waiting to launch his fallaway jumper over an imaginary opponent.

(Preceding page) Olajuwon (34) shoots over the Knicks' Charles Oakley (34) at The Summit in Houston during Game 7 of the NBA Finals. Olajuwon was named the 1994 Finals MVP after averaging 26.9 points, 9.1 rebounds, 3.6 assists and 3.9 blocks during the seven-game series. (Above) Tomjanovich was promoted from Rockets' assistant coach to interim head coach late in the 1991-92 season and was given the permanent job for 1992-93. The former Houston star player led the Rockets to back-to-back NBA titles in 1994 and 1995.

Without a doubt, Olajuwon was the most graceful big man to ever play the game. But he needed more than grace to beat the rough, tough Knicks. Charles Oakley, Anthony Mason and Ewing would meet his mastery with forearm shivers. To overcome them, Tomjanovich knew he was going to have to keep the floor spread and use his 3-point shooters to make New York pay for double-teaming Olajuwon.

The championship series would run the full seven games for the first time since the Pistons and Lakers had battled in 1988. To the Rockets' advantage, the previous 19 times that a playoff series had gone to seven games in the NBA, the home team had won. And 11 of the 14 previous NBA Finals to go to a seventh game had been claimed by the home club.

Just about all parties agreed that a showdown between these two great centers should come to a seventh game. Olajuwon, the first pick in the 1984 NBA Draft, and Ewing, the first pick in '85, had faced each other 22 times previously in their pro careers. The Rockets had won 13 of those games.

Both were asked if their place in history would be decided by the outcome. "I don't think my career will be defined by it," Ewing said. "I'll be disappointed if we don't win. That's it."

"I'm not playing for my place in history," Olajuwon said. "I just don't know any other way to play than to play to win."

With this background, Game 7 unfolded much like the six others that preceded it. The Knicks challenged, and the Rockets looked for room to work. Ultimately, they found it. Olajuwon scored 25 and Maxwell finished with 21, plus great defense on New York's John Starks.

Cassell, too, played a huge game, scoring 8 of his 13 points in the fourth as the Rockets claimed their first title with a 90-84 victory.

"If you write a book, you can't write it any better," said Olajuwon, the Finals MVP.

The next season, the Rockets would make a trade at midseason for Olajuwon's old college teammate, Clyde Drexler, and despite the issues of trying to assemble a new chemistry on short notice, they would win a second championship — the two cornerstones of Olajuwon's Hall-of-Fame career.

2007-08 BOSTON CELTICS

After winning NBA titles in the 1950s, '60s, '70s and '80s, the great Boston Celtics franchise took a prolonged vacation from the spotlight. The Celtics claimed the 1986 championship, and then lost the next season in the NBA Finals. What followed was 20 years of decline that included a revolving door of players, coaches, executives and owners.

Midway through the first decade of the new century, former Boston great Danny Ainge was running the club, and his coach was an old foe, Doc Rivers, who had once battled Boston as a point guard for the Atlanta Hawks. They were great

2007-08 Boston Celtics

Coach: Glenn "Doc" Rivers

No.	Player	Pos.	Ht.	Wt.
20	Ray Allen	G	6-5	205
42	Tony Allen	G	6-4	213
93	P.J. Brown	F-C	6-11	225
28	Sam Cassell	G	6-3	185
11	Glen Davis	F	6-9	289
5	Kevin Garnett	F	6-11	220
50	Eddie House	G	6-1	180
43	Kendrick Perkins	C	6-10	280
34	Paul Pierce	F	6-6	230
66	Scot Pollard	C	6-11	265
41	James Posey	F-G	6-8	215
0	Leon Powe	F	6-8	240
13	Gabe Pruitt	G	6-4	170
9	Rajon Rondo	G	6-1	171
44	Brian Scalabrine	F	6-9	241

Team Stats

PTS	PPG	REB	RPG	AST	APG
8,245	100.5	3,445	42.0	1,833	22.4

Regular Season
66-16; First Place – Atlantic Division

Playoffs
Eastern Conference First Round:
    Beat Atlanta Hawks 4-3
Eastern Conference Semifinals:
    Beat Cleveland Cavaliers 4-3
Eastern Conference Finals:
    Beat Detroit Pistons 4-2
NBA Finals: Beat Los Angeles Lakers 4-2

(Preceding page, and left) The 2007-08 Boston Celtics. Front row (from left): Kevin Garnett, Paul Pierce, Glenn "Doc" Rivers (head coach), Robert Epstein (managing partner), Stephen Pagliuca (managing partner), Wycliffe Grousebeck (managing partner/governor), H. Irving Grousbeck (managing partner), Danny Ainge (president of basketball operations), Rich Gotham (president), Ray Allen, James Posey. Middle row (from left): John Connor (team travel/equipment manager), Phil Lynch (director of team security), Eddie House, Tony Allen, Brandon Wallace, Glen Davis, Brian Scalabrine, Kendrick Perkins, Scot Pollard, Leon Powe, Rajon Rondo, Gabe Pruitt, Ed Lacerte (head athletic trainer), Vladimir Shulman (massage therapist). Back row (from left): Brian Adams (video coordinator), Bryan Doo (strength and conditioning coach), Walter Norton Jr. (strength and conditioning coach), Michael Longabardi (assistant coach), Kevin Eastman (assistant coach), Clifford Ray (assistant coach), Armond Hill (assistant coach), Tom Thibodeau (associate head coach), Dr. Brian McKeon (team physician), Michael Crotty (director of player development), Darren Erman (coaching assistant).

friends, but their tenure with the team seemed in doubt until the magical offseason of 2007, when a mother lode of talent arrived in Beantown.

First, Ainge landed perennial All-Star Ray Allen from Seattle on the night of the NBA Draft. Then five weeks later Minnesota Timberwolves executive Kevin McHale, Ainge's old Celtics teammate, agreed to trade Kevin Garnett to Boston. The Celtics gave up four of their top five scorers from 2007 — and seven players in all — but held onto perennial All-Star Paul Pierce. Garnett, Allen and Pierce were quickly dubbed the "Big Three," a modern take on the Celtics' star trio from the '80s — Larry Bird, Robert Parish and McHale.

Many Boston enthusiasts proclaimed the team ready to take the Eastern Conference title before the season even started. But others questioned the newcomers' age (Allen was already 32 and Garnett soon would be) and the new Celtics' lack of chemistry. Each had been the primary option on their previous teams and it would take time for Pierce, Allen and Garnett to learn to play together and to accommodate each other on the floor.

"We still have to work on chemistry and bonding," Garnett said, "[but] we are going to be a force to be reckoned with."

Pierce had talked of being traded, but that quieted immediately with the upgrades.

"I asked for veterans," he said. "I didn't expect to get a seven-time All-Star and a 10-time All-Star. This is a dream come true. I feel like a rookie again. I couldn't ask for a better situation."

That "situation" would lead to the greatest turnaround in NBA history, going from 24 wins in 2007 to a league-best 66 in 2008. With each victory the already burgeoning expectations grew some more. The Celtics rolled through their first eight games, and fans began to see that the team's youth — center Kendrick Perkins and point guard Rajon Rondo — would play important roles. With veteran assistant coach Clifford Ray doing the tutoring, Perkins began developing into a strong low-post defender and rebounder.

And Rondo was on his way to proving that he could be a game-changer at the point, even though he lacked an outside shot.

"Once I saw how hard he worked every day," Garnett said of Rondo, "I just knew this kid was going to be great."

Another key factor would be reserves James Posey and Eddie House, who made Boston's depth something other teams feared.

The Celtics got home wins over Denver, the Los Angeles Lakers and Golden State, but that only raised questions about how they would fare on the road against the stronger Western Conference.

They met that question head on in late December, winning four games in five nights against Sacramento, Seattle, Utah and the Lakers. The last two victories were particularly strong. They wound up 25-5 overall against the West and cruised down the stretch to earn home-court advantage throughout the playoffs. That was a good thing, because they would need it — even in the first round against an Atlanta team that had finished 29 games behind them in the standings. The Celtics didn't win a road game in the opening two rounds, moving past the Hawks and Cleveland by staying strong on the parquet in Boston.

"When you look at it, some of the problems were kind of to be expected," said Rivers. "It was our first time together as a playoff team, and we had to see how we were going to react to that."

They finally got two road wins while dismissing Detroit in six games in the Eastern Conference Finals. Like that, for the first time in two decades, the men in green were headed back to the

(Preceding page) Garnett (5) moves around Lakers defender Pau Gasol for a basket during Game 4 of the 2008 NBA Finals in Los Angeles. Garnett averaged 18.2 points per game during the six-game series. (Right) The "Big Three" of Allen, Garnett and Pierce graced the front cover of the Celtics' 2007-08 media guide.

the game, all of which was celebrated uproariously by the Garden crowd.

"Beat LA," the fans chanted over and over.

No problem, said the Celtics.

They went on to pound Los Angeles in six games, including a historic comeback in Game 4 that drew almost 15 million television viewers on ABC.

The Celtics sprinted from 20 points down with five minutes to go in the third period to take a commanding 3-1 lead with a 97-91 victory led by reserves Posey and House.

The Celtics produced an even worse nightmare for the Lakers while closing out the series in Game 6. After a rocky first quarter, Boston dominated the rest of the game. Maintaining a lead of more than 25 points, the Celtics' Big Three took charge, while Boston's team defense fairly smothered the famed LA triangle. The telling stat was Boston's 48-29 edge in rebounds with a 14-2 disparity on the offensive glass.

Allen hit seven 3-pointers to tie what was then the Finals record (which he would later break in Game 2 of the 2010 NBA Finals). Rondo filled out the stat sheet with 21 points, eight rebounds, seven assists and six steals. Boston set a Finals record with 18 steals, and the 39-point margin of victory was the largest ever in an NBA title-clinching game, breaking the old record of 33, also set by the Celtics over the Lakers in Game 5 of the 1965 series.

Their 17th title extended their record by a team for most championships, although it had followed the long dry spell. And they upped their dominance against the Lakers to 9-2 in championship meetings, 24 years since their last victory over LA in 1984.

Injuries would derail this Boston train the next season, but Garnett, Pierce and Allen would drive the team to another championship meeting with the Lakers in 2010, won by Los Angeles in a remarkable Game 7. There was little question that Boston's second edition of the Big Three was one of the hardest-competing teams in pro basketball history.

championship series. And their opponents would be Phil Jackson's Lakers, the 11th time the two franchises had met for the title.

The Celtics had to look no farther than the rafters of TD Banknorth Garden — as the Fleet Center had been renamed — to find their inspiration.

"Well, when you look at all the retired members up on the banner, all of them except one (Reggie Lewis) has a ring," said Pierce. "So I think so, man, in order to be great — in order to be a legend — you have to win a championship."

"We've got our eyes on the prize," Perkins told reporters.

The championship series opened June 5, 2008, in Boston, with the Lakers as favorites. Game 1 will be forever known as the wheelchair game, when Pierce was rolled back into the arena after a knee injury sidelined him in the third quarter. Despite a knee strain, he returned to the game and hit the big shots that drove a 98-88 Celtics win. A pattern of sorts was established early in the first quarter of that first game. Using their triangle offense, with Kobe Bryant working from the wing, the Lakers took advantage of Boston's overplaying defense to score on a series of back cuts.

However, the Boston coaching staff quickly adjusted at halftime by packing their defense back in the lane and putting the triangle on ice.

With their star in check, the Lakers ground to a halt and stood around confused as the Celtics ruled the boards (a 46-33 edge) and

(Top left) Rivers smoked a victory cigar in 2008 in front of a portrait of Celtics patriarch Red Auerbach, who led the franchise to 16 titles before his passing in 2006. (Opposite page) Pierce holds up his 2008 NBA Finals MVP Award after Celtics beat the Lakers in six games. Pierce averaged 21.8 points in the series.

1967 World Cha...

1966-67 PHILADELPHIA 76ERS

The scope of Wilt Chamberlain's greatness will always remain one of basketball's hottest debates. Those who list him at the height of the hoops pantheon always point to the 1966-67 Philadelphia 76ers as one of the greatest teams of all time. His detractors — including those who played with and against him — don't hold that Sixers club in quite the same esteem.

The club did finish the year at 68-13, which at the time was the most wins ever by an NBA team. But with the league expanding in the late 1960s, the record lasted only a couple of seasons.

Wilt's Sixers team only had that one dominant season. Otherwise, his career was marked largely by giant frustration.

1966-67 Philadelphia 76ers

Coach: Alex Hannum

No.	Player	Pos.	Ht.	Wt.
13	Wilt Chamberlain	C	7-1	275
21	Larry Costello	G	6-1	186
32	Billy Cunningham	F-C	6-6	210
20	Dave Gambee	F	6-6	215
15	Hal Greer	G-F	6-2	175
14	Matt Guokas	G-F	6-5	175
54	Luke Jackson	F-C	6-9	240
24	Wali Jones	G	6-2	180
28	Bill Melchionni	G	6-1	165
25	Chet Walker	F-G	6-6	212
12	Bob Weiss	G	6-2	180

Team Stats

PTS	PPG	REB	RPG	AST	APG
10,143	125.2	5,701	70.4	2,138	26.4

Regular Season
68-13; First Place – Eastern Division

Playoffs
Eastern Conference Semifinals:
     Beat Cincinnati Royals 3-1
Eastern Conference Finals:
     Beat Boston Celtics 4-1
NBA Finals: Beat San Francisco Warriors 4-2

(Preceding page, and left) The 1966-67 Philadelphia 76ers. Front row (from left): Wilt Chamberlain, Dave Gambee, Lucious Jackson, Billy Cunningham, Chet Walker. Back row (from left): Al Domenico (trainer), Alex Hannum (head coach), Wali Jones, Bill Melchionni, Matt Guokas, Hal Greer, Larry Costello, Irv Kosloff (owner), general manager Jack Ramsay.

Chamberlain came close to winning an NCAA championship in 1957, but his University of Kansas Jayhawks lost to North Carolina in triple overtime in the title game.

The giant would travel across a decade and swim a sea of ridicule before he finally gained his coveted championship ring in 1967. True, he was a stats monster, but little else.

He came to the NBA in 1959-60 in a heralded return to his hometown Philadelphia to play for the old Warriors. His presence had an immediate impact on the league's statistical races. He led the NBA in scoring (37.6 points per game) and rebounding (27 per game).

The next season, 1961-62, he became the first player in league history to shoot better than 50 percent from the floor. Oh, and he maximized man's potential for 48 minutes of basketball by averaging 50.4 points per game. The next season, he scored a mere 44.8 points per game and won the league rebounding title for the fourth straight season.

Each season he achieved these wonderful things, and yet each season ended in bitter disappointment. The reason, of course, was the Boston Celtics. Quite often Chamberlain would dominate Bill Russell statistically, but he could never vanquish the Boston center and his teammates in the big games. Chamberlain was actually taller than his listed height of 7-foot-1 and towered over the 6-foot-9 Russell. To the basketball public, Russell had a winner's heart, while Chamberlain certainly lacked something.

In truth, Russell was simply quicker than Chamberlain, according to Boston's Hall of Fame point guard Bob Cousy, repeating a view that was held by insiders.

"This is a tremendous advantage Russell had on Wilt," Cousy said. "He didn't give him the offensive position he wanted. Russell kept him from overpowering him and going to the basket. Russell had better speed and quickness, so he could always beat Wilt to the spot. He pushed Chamberlain out a little farther from the basket, forcing him to put the ball on the floor once or twice. We always felt Russell could handle him one-on-one."

As a result, Chamberlain was forced to develop and shoot a fall-away jumper that was far less effective than his dunks and short bank shots. In the public's mind, it was simply a case of a giant failing to live up to his ability.

Cousy agreed with those critics. "Wilt's a nice man," he said, "but I don't think he ever understood why four other people were running around the floor with him."

"It's interesting those things about him people would misinterpret," Jerry West said of Chamberlain. "They would say he was a selfish guy, that he didn't care, that he wasn't a team player. And that simply was not the truth. He's like all of us. No athlete wants to fail. Wilt Chamberlain certainly didn't want to."

The Warriors moved to San Francisco for 1962-63, and Chamberlain continued to lead the league in scoring. The following season, he broadened the scope of his game by finishing fifth in assists. It didn't matter. The Warriors lost in the 1964 NBA Finals 4-1 to Russell and the Celtics.

Frustrated, San Francisco traded Chamberlain in the middle of the next season to Philadelphia, where he quickly made the 76ers into a title contender. But that spring they lost a seven-game series to the Celtics again. The following year, Philadelphia actually beat out Boston for the Eastern Division's regular-season crown, but they were caught flat-footed in the Eastern playoffs and lost 4-1 to the Celtics.

After losing in the 1966 playoffs, the 76ers fired coach Dolph Schayes and hired Alex Hannum, Chamberlain's former coach in San Francisco. Where Chamberlain disregarded most coaching, he respected Hannum and listened to him.

The Celtics won 60 games in 1966-67, tying the second-highest total in their illustrious history. However, that was eight games behind Chamberlain and the 76ers. Philly opened the season by winning 15 of their first 16, losing only a road game at the Cincinnati Royals. That was followed by an 11-game winning streak, then a loss to the New York Knicks, then another streak that brought their record to 37-3. Another win streak took it to 46-4.

"That whole season was just magical, something where a team played almost perfect basketball," sharp-shooting guard Wali Jones recalled. "We played as a team/family concept."

(Opposite page) Chamberlain (13) brings down a rebound in front of the Celtics' Bill Russell (6) while Philadelphia's Cunningham (32) and Greer (15) and Boston's John Havlicek (17) watch during the 1967 NBA championship series in Boston. Chamberlain averaged 21.7 points and 29.1 rebounds during the playoffs.

If it was a family, it was a prolific one. They averaged 125.2 points per game. But for the first time in his career, Chamberlain wasn't the big daddy. He averaged a career-low 24.1 points per game. As he had in San Francisco, Hannum had persuaded Chamberlain to concentrate less on scoring and more on rebounding and defense. He again led the league in boards at 24.2 per game, plus he shot an unfathomable 68.3 percent from the floor, a league record. And he was third in the league in assists at 7.8 per game.

Hannum also lured Larry Costello out of retirement to help in the backcourt, where Jones and Hal Greer were the starters.

The Sixers took up Chamberlain's offensive slack with balance, with six people scoring in double figures. Greer averaged 22.1 points a game, and Jones was good for 13.2. While the backcourt was merely excellent, the frontcourt was incredible. Chet Walker, the fifth-year forward out of Bradley, averaged 19.3 points. Reserve Billy Cunningham, in his second year out of North Carolina, scored at an 18.5 clip. And Lucious Jackson did the rest of the power work on the boards plus averaged 12 points a game. Jackson was 6-foot-9, 240 pounds, and sported an almost-shaven head — the picture of an intimidator.

Rookie Matt Guokas Jr. came on strong as the team's third guard at the close of the season.

Their 68-13 record was nice, but the real golden moment came when they blew past the Celtics 4-1 in the Eastern Finals. From there, they went on to push past Rick Barry and the Warriors in the NBA championship series in six games.

1967 Philadelphia 76ers

FRONT ROW: Wilt Chamberlain, Dave Gambee, Luke Jackson, Bill Cunningham, Chet Walker
STANDING: Al Domenico, Trainer; Alex Hannum, Coach; Wally Jones, Bill Melchionni, Matt Guokas, Hal Greer, Larry Costello; Irv Kosloff, President; Jack Ramsay, General Manager

At last, the Sixers had gotten their champagne. They took turns pouring it over Hannum's bald head. The spotlight, though, belonged to Chamberlain. No longer could the basketball public say "the Stilt" was a loser.

Jones had grown up in Philadelphia idolizing Chamberlain. "Everyone who knows the game of basketball, knows who really is the greatest," he said.

(Preceding page) Greer sets up for a jump shot against the Celtics during the 1967 NBA Finals in Boston. Greer led the 76ers in scoring during the 1967 playoffs with a 27.7 point average. (Preceding page right, and left) Hannum was brought in as Philadelphia's head coach for the 1966-67 season, and Chamberlain and the 76ers responded with a title.

1973-74
BOSTON CELTICS

After leading the Celtics through a run of championships, Bill Russell retired in 1969, and Boston spent a couple of brief seasons in basketball purgatory.

Then Red Auerbach rebuilt again around the great John Havlicek. The Celtics drafted Donald "Duck" Chaney out of the University of Houston in 1968, and the next year they got Jo Jo White from the University of Kansas. Both players would require a little seasoning, but before long, the pair would make a splendid backcourt.

Auerbach's real coup, though, was at center. Boston selected Florida State's Dave Cowens as the fourth player in the first round of the 1970 NBA Draft, only the Celtics' general manager wasn't quite sure what to do with him. He figured that at 6-foot-9, Cowens was too short to be an NBA center. But in training camp later that summer, Cowens

1973-74 Boston Celtics

Coach: Tom Heinsohn

No.	Player	Pos.	Ht.	Wt.
12	Don Chaney	G	6-5	210
18	Dave Cowens	C-F	6-9	230
32	Steve Downing	C	6-8	225
29	Hank Finkel	C	7-0	240
20	Phil Hankinson	F	6-8	195
17	John Havlicek	F-G	6-5	203
11	Steve Kuberski	F-C	6-8	215
19	Don Nelson	F	6-6	210
35	Paul Silas	F-C	6-7	220
44	Paul Westphal	G	6-4	195
10	Jo Jo White	G	6-3	190
7	Art Williams	G	6-1	180

Team Stats

PTS	PPG	REB	RPG	AST	APG
8,937	109.0	4,452	54.3	2,187	26.7

Regular Season
56-26; First Place – Atlantic Division

Playoffs
Eastern Conference Semifinals:
    Beat Buffalo Braves 4-2
Eastern Conference Finals:
    Beat New York Knicks 4-1
NBA Finals: Beat Milwaukee Bucks 4-3

(Preceding page, and left) The 1973-74 Boston Celtics. Front row (from left): Jo Jo White, Don Chaney, John Havlicek, Red Auerbach (president/GM), Robert Schmertz (chairman of the board), Tom Heinsohn (head coach), Dave Cowens, Paul Silas, John Killilea (assistant coach). Back row (from left): Mark Volk (assistant trainer), Dr. Samuel Kane (team dentist), Paul Westphal, Phil Hankinson, Steve Downing, Don Nelson, Hank Finkel, Steve Kuberski, Art Williams, Dr. Thomas Silva (team physician), Frank Challant (trainer).

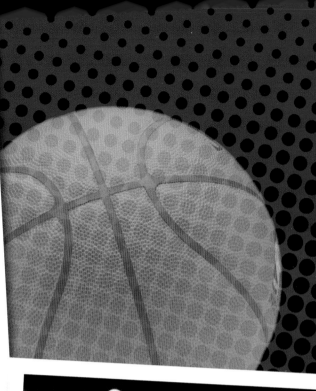

resisted being moved to forward. Auerbach struggled with the problem, then decided to phone Bill Russell for a bit of advice.

Let him play where he wants, Russell told Auerbach. "No one's going to intimidate that kid."

It didn't take Auerbach long to see what Russell was talking about. Cowens scored 33 points and grabbed 22 rebounds against Wilt Chamberlain during an exhibition game before the 1970-71 season. That and his performance in several summer league games convinced the Celtics brass that he could be a center. Given the chance, Cowens played the position the way no one ever had before. He was too small to bang around in the low post with his larger opponents. So he used his other assets. He was a fine leaper and he had great speed and long arms. More importantly, he showed the aggressiveness of a linebacker.

"I don't worry about injuries," he said cockily. "I'm the one going a little bit nutty out there."

His speed and agility allowed him to play corner-to-corner. It also meant that the Celtics had the best switching defense in the league, because Cowens could switch to a smaller man and not lose a step. "He adds a different dimension to Boston's game," Chicago's Norm Van Lier said not long after Cowens came into the league. "He has a great defensive range on a horizontal rather than a vertical plane. He'll meet me at the top of the key, spread those long arms and make it almost impossible to pass off."

Over time, Cowens proved he could neutralize the giants of his era — Kareem Abdul-Jabbar, Wilt Chamberlain, Bob Lanier and Nate Thurmond — with his quickness. "He's so quick he's like a 6-foot-9 Jerry West," said Jerry Lucas of the Knicks. "One minute he's standing in front of you and the next he's gone, rolling in toward the basket or straight up in the air shooting his jumper. It's like he disappears."

Tommy Heinsohn, the erstwhile gunner, had followed Russell as the Celtics' coach. Heinsohn's goal was to make them a running

(Preceding page, left) Cowens (18) battles Milwaukee star center Kareem Abdul-Jabbar (33) for position during the 1974 NBA Finals in Boston. Cowens' defensive effort on Abdul-Jabbar in Game 7 helped give the Celtics the title. (Preceding page, bottom right) Heinsohn, after a Hall-of-Fame playing career with the Celtics, took over as coach in 1969-70 and led Boston to a pair of NBA titles. (Right) Havlicek was the 1974 Finals MVP after averaging 26.4 points against Milwaukee.

team again, and Cowens was perfect for it. Heinsohn figured Cowens was faster in the 100-yard dash than any player in the league.

But Cowens couldn't solve all of Heinsohn's problems. He faced the task of getting the old Celtics to accept the new batch of youngsters. Eventually the Boston newcomers would mix well with the holdovers from the Russell years — Havlicek, Don Nelson and Satch Sanders. Heinsohn's major developmental work involved the guards. With long arms and a nose for steals, the 6-foot-5 Chaney was a solid defensive guard, and White ran the Boston break.

This new edition of the Celtics wasn't pretty, but it was a winner. They nailed down 44 games in 1971 and 56 in 1972, making their progress obvious.

Then, just before the 1972-73 season, Auerbach obtained Paul Silas from Phoenix, and the team had just the power forward it needed. An eight-year pro, Silas had trimmed to a svelte 6-foot-7, 230-pounder and was ready to join Heinsohn's version of the Boston marathon. He came in that first season and played like a charm, albeit a bullish one. Silas pulled down 1,039 rebounds (13 per game), while Cowens got 1,329, making Boston the best board team in the league. It was the first time in league history that two teammates had each grabbed 1,000 rebounds.

All that defensive rebounding, of course, was just what the doctor ordered for Heinsohn's running game. The Celtics ran off to a 68-14 record, the best in the club's distinguished history. But then an unprecedented thing happened in Boston. The two best teams in basketball, the Celtics and the Knicks, met in the Eastern Conference

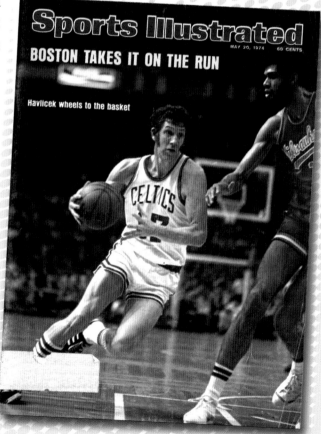

Finals, and in the decisive seventh game, in Boston Garden no less, the Celtics stumbled. They lost and watched New York go on to trample Los Angeles for the world championship.

It was a bitter, bitter ending to a bright beginning.

As Boston fans hoped, the Celtics opened the 1973-74 season with a vengeance, racing out to a 30-7 start. From there, though, they grew strangely complacent and barely played .500 ball over the remainder of the schedule.

Fortunately, they had the luck of the Irish with them. The Eastern Conference was a bit weak with the Knicks aging and injured. Boston finished 56-26, good enough for the best record in the conference, but short of Milwaukee's 59-33 mark in the West. Still, the Celtics powered their way past the Buffalo Braves and New York in the Eastern playoffs and advanced to the NBA Finals for the first time ever without Russell.

Milwaukee moved just as surely in the Western Conference, dropping Los Angeles 4-1, then Chicago 4-0 in the Conference Finals, which meant the two best teams in the pro game would battle for the title. Their matchup was an invigorating clash of styles. With Abdul-Jabbar and his famed skyhook, the Bucks were the consummate half-court team and nearly unstoppable when the big center got the ball in the post. On the other hand, the Celtics were a small, quick, pressing and running team that approached things from basic simplicity. Their starting front line ran 6-foot-7, 6-foot-8 and 6-foot-5. Heinsohn knew if his troops were going to win, the press would have to do it for them. They'd have to take the ball away before the Bucks ever got it upcourt to Kareem.

So they put a lot of ball pressure on 35-year-old Oscar Robertson and found just enough of an edge to win a dramatic championship series with a great Milwaukee team.

The basketball purists also relished the idea of the small, quick Cowens meeting the giant, athletic Abdul-Jabbar in the Finals. Under the Celtics' scheme, they would leave their center to fend for himself man-to-man. As a rookie, Cowens had watched helplessly as Kareem scored 53 against him. "No one wants to look used and foolish out on the court," Cowens told the writers covering the Finals. "Our style doesn't give me much help. But I have a couple of things going for me. When the guys are off pressing, they're really helping me. The better they press, the less often Kareem's going to get the ball."

That, in short, became a blueprint for the series, the basis on which each team made its adjustments. It quickly developed into one of the most engrossing championship rounds in league history, one in which the home-court advantage meant almost nothing.

The Celtics wasted little time in taking a 1-0 lead with a Game 1 win in Milwaukee. The series featured a double-overtime Game 6, won by a Kareem skyhook.

Then Cowens scored 28 with 14 rebounds and an incalculable defensive effort on Abdul-Jabbar to drive Boston to a Game 7 victory in Milwaukee.

Soaked in pink champagne, Cowens grinned broadly in the Celtics' locker room afterward and accepted the MVP award. This young team had finally lived up to his standards and Russell's tradition. Back in Boston, they were shifting things around in the Garden rafters to make room for title banner No. 12.

(Opposite page) Silas (35) harassed Milwaukee's Oscar Robertson (1) during the 1974 NBA Finals, holding him to 12 points per game in the seven-game series. Silas and Cowens combined to make Boston one of the best rebounding teams in the NBA.

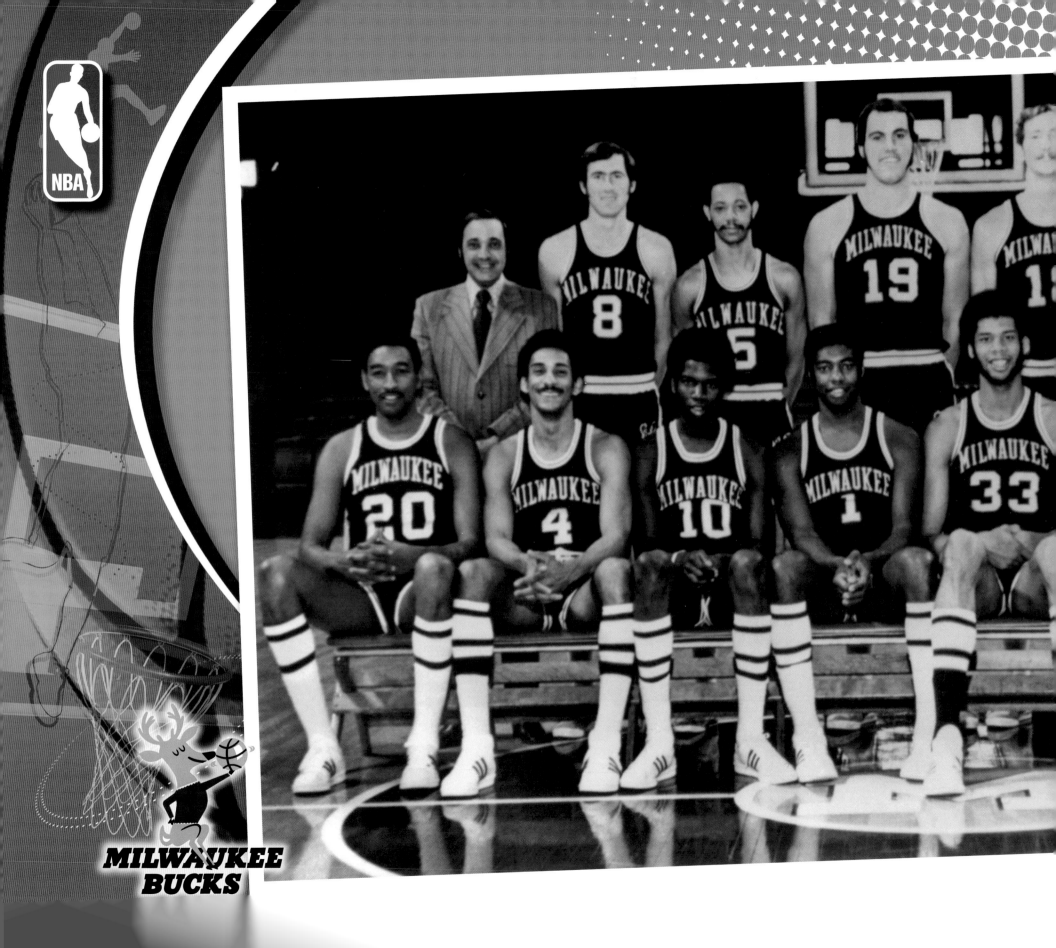

NBA

MILWAUKEE
BUCKS

1970-71 MILWAUKEE BUCKS

Over the years, the language of basketball has settled on the term "the complete player" to describe the ultimate, the best. It means the guy who can do everything. Shoot. Dribble. Pass. Rebound. Play defense. Win.

In other words: Oscar Robertson.

"In his time, he was the greatest," said Ed Jucker, a former coach at the University of Cincinnati. "No one was the equal to him. ... He could play any position."

Not only was Robertson complete, but he was almost nonchalant about it, former University of Kansas coach Dick Harp said. "He had unbelievable control of a basketball game, and many times he looked like he was taking a walk in the country when he did it. He was so much in control of things. He had the size, the quickness, everything. He had all those great blessings, but among them he had great judgment about what to do with the ball."

1970-71 Milwaukee Bucks

Coach: Larry Costello

No.	Player	Pos.	Ht.	Wt.
33	Lew Alcindor	C	7-2	225
7	Lucius Allen	G	6-2	175
20	Bob Boozer	F	6-8	215
19	Dick Cunningham	C	6-10	245
10	Bob Dandridge	F-G	6-6	195
17-27	Gary Freeman	F	6-9	210
18	Bob Greacen	F	6-7	206
14	Jon McGlocklin	G-F	6-5	205
35	McCoy McLemore	F-C	6-7	230
1	Oscar Robertson	G-F	6-5	205
4	Greg Smith	F	6-5	195
8	Jeff Webb	G	6-4	170
5	Marv Winkler	G	6-1	164
6	Bill Zopf	G	6-1	170

Team Stats

PTS	PPG	REB	RPG	AST	APG
9,710	118.4	4,344	53.0	2,249	27.4

Regular Season
66-16; First Place – Midwest Division

Playoffs
Western Conference Semifinals:
    Beat San Francisco Warriors 4-1
Western Conference Finals:
    Beat Los Angeles Lakers 4-1
NBA Finals: Beat Baltimore Bullets 4-0

(Preceding page, and left) The 1970-71 Milwaukee Bucks. Front row (from left): Bob Boozer, Greg Smith, Bob Dandridge, Oscar Robertson, Lew Alcindor, Jon McGlocklin, Lucius Allen, Larry Costello (head coach). Back row (from left): Arnie Garber (trainer), Jeff Webb, Marv Winkler, Dick Cunningham, Bob Greacen, McCoy McLemore, Tom Nissalke (assistant coach).

Ultimately, however, the question for players like Jordan, Bird and Robertson is not how complete they make themselves, but how complete they make their teams.

The top pick of the 1960 NBA Draft, Robertson was the heart and soul of the Cincinnati Royals for the first 10 years of his pro career. Despite making the playoffs several times, the Royals never advanced to the NBA Finals.

Then in 1970, Robertson was traded to the Milwaukee Bucks, a three-year-old team with a future. The future was one Lew Alcindor, the 7-foot-2 center who was about to change his name to Kareem Abdul-Jabbar after converting to Islam. His career stood in direct contrast to Robertson's. Alcindor's UCLA teams had won three straight NCAA titles. In fact, his biggest adjustment as a Bucks rookie during the 1969-70 season had been learning how to lose.

John Wooden often said Alcindor was the most valuable college player ever. The UCLA coach emphasized that Alcindor was the kind of gifted, versatile player who could take a team beyond the sum of its players. Winning was almost the nonchalant byproduct of Alcindor's businesslike approach to the game. That made him a perfect match for Robertson.

"He wants that championship," Alcindor explained to reporters later. "Me, I've got some time, but Oscar wants it right now. Right this year. And he's got us all feeling that way."

Robertson's reputation around the league was Oscar the Grouch, the guy who would blister you right out on the court if you weren't hustling. He respected those who could perform, but if you didn't keep up, watch out.

That attitude worked well in Milwaukee, where the Bucks had set a record for rapidly assembling a team. With general manager Ray Patterson, it was trade city. "We got Lucius Allen in a trade," Robertson said. "We got Bob Boozer in a trade. I went there in a trade."

And just about all of those who hadn't come in a trade were brand new. Bobby Dandridge, a 6-foot-6 forward out of Norfolk

Some observers like to compare Robertson to the big-name modern-day players, Magic Johnson or Michael Jordan. But Pete Newell, the former pro and college coach, says Robertson actually has more in common with Larry Bird. Most people think of Robertson as a guard, Newell said, because he played guard as a professional. But in college at Cincinnati, Robertson was a forward.

"Oscar played forward more like Larry Bird plays forward," Newell said. "He was such a great passer. He brought the ball up even though he was playing forward. He was so tough when he got the ball. Oscar would go down and get it. Then they'd clear for him, and he'd just take it on his own. There was no way you could stop Oscar one-on-one from penetrating and getting his shot."

(Top left) Costello was named Milwaukee's head coach for the franchise's inaugural season of 1968-69. Three seasons later, the Bucks were the NBA champions with the first Finals sweep since 1959. (Opposite page) Robertson (1) takes a jumper over Baltimore Bullets guard Fred Carter (3) during the 1971 NBA Finals in Milwaukee. Robertson averaged 19.4 points during the regular season and 23.5 points in the four-game sweep of the Bullets.

State, had been selected in the fourth round of the 1969 NBA Draft. He and Alcindor had earned all-rookie first-team honors for the 1969-70 season. Allen was a second-year player, too, having been obtained from Seattle. Greg Smith, the other starting forward, was only in his third year out of Western Kentucky.

The veterans were solid. Jon McGlocklin, a sixth-year player out of Indiana, started alongside Robertson in the backcourt, where he averaged 15.8 points per game while shooting 53.5 percent from the floor. Boozer, also obtained from Seattle, was the major frontcourt substitute. Both Boozer and McGlocklin had played with Robertson in Cincinnati.

With 17 teams, the NBA was now organized into four divisions, and Milwaukee dominated all four with a league-best 66-16 record. At one point, they won 20 straight, breaking the Knicks' year-old record for consecutive wins.

Robertson's scoring average, usually above 30 during his years in Cincinnati, dipped to 19.4, as he spent his time running the team and sending the ball down low to the big man. That worked. Alcindor led the league in scoring at 31.7 points and was named MVP.

By season's end, the Bucks had become machinelike in their efficiency, which was exactly what coach Larry Costello had sought. A 12-year pro himself, Costello had been hired three seasons earlier when the team formed. With Costello, Robertson and Alcindor, the atmosphere was all business.

(Left) Alcindor, who changed his name to Kareem Abdul-Jabbar after the season, takes a free throw in Baltimore during the 1971 NBA Finals. Alcindor was the NBA's MVP for 1970-71, and his 27 points and 18.5 rebounds against the Bullets earned him Finals MVP honors as part of a Hall-of-Fame career. (Opposite page) Robertson is considered one of basketball's greatest players, both in college at the University of Cincinnati and the NBA with the Bucks and Cincinnati Royals.

"Larry, Oscar and I have the same ways about us," Alcindor told reporters as the season came to a close. "We agree that being as efficient as possible cuts down on our chances for errors."

This emphasis on execution made Milwaukee one of the greatest offensive teams in league history. They led the league in scoring, yet were only 12th in field goals attempted. And they were the first team in league history to average better than 50 percent from the field.

In the playoffs, the Bucks promptly dusted San Francisco 4-1 in the first round. They lost their only game to the Warriors when sub Joe Ellis hit a 43-foot buzzer beater. The Chicago Bulls with Bob Love, Chet Walker and Jerry Sloan provided some trouble at the next level but eventually fell 4-3.

The Bucks advanced to meet the Lakers in the Western Finals, but it wasn't the same Los Angeles team of a year earlier. Jerry West and Elgin Baylor were out with injuries, and with Wilt Chamberlain as the focal point, Los Angeles had become a plodding half-court team. Milwaukee pushed them aside 4-1.

All along, the Bucks had their eyes on the Eastern, where the Knicks were embroiled in a tight fight with the Baltimore Bullets. With Willis Reed bullying Alcindor, the Knicks had taken a 4-1 edge in their regular-season series with Milwaukee. But the matchup was not to be. Baltimore outlasted New York in a seven-game Eastern Final, a development that deeply disappointed the Bucks. The Bullets were no match for Milwaukee. Baltimore center Wes Unseld had badly sprained his ankle as the season ended and was supposed to be out six weeks. Somehow he hobbled back for the playoffs.

With the Bullets' offense hurting, the Bucks squeezed a defensive noose around the games. Baltimore would shoot better than 40 percent in only one game in the series. And in only two quarters did they score more than 30 points. The result was only the second sweep in Finals history, the other being the Celtics over Minneapolis in 1959.

"It was almost like pure basketball," Robertson said years later. At the time, the writers and fans thought they were witnessing the birth of another dynasty. Instead, Milwaukee management broke up the team.

"After the championship, they did something which was really foolish," Robertson said. "They traded Greg Smith, Bob Boozer and Dick Cunningham. You had people who really did not understand what a team concept means. You win a championship and make a trade of any key ballplayer, and it's the kiss of death."

1976-77 PORTLAND TRAIL BLAZERS

In three years of varsity competition, Bill Walton led UCLA to two NCAA championships and 88 consecutive wins, smashing the 60-game streak set by Bill Russell's teams at the University of San Francisco. Walton also set UCLA's career assist record, which left observers declaring him the best passing center in the history of the game.

His college performance led to projections that Walton would be pro basketball's next dominant player. Those dreams would go largely unfulfilled due to a series of foot injuries, but for one bright shining season in 1976-77 he led the Portland Trail Blazers to a storybook NBA championship.

The coach of that Blazers team, Dr. Jack Ramsay, would go on to spend

1976-77 Portland Trail Blazers

Coach: Jack Ramsay

No.	Player	Pos.	Ht.	Wt.
10	Corky Calhoun	F	6-7	210
16	Johnny Davis	G	6-2	170
3	Herm Gilliam	G-F	6-3	190
30	Bob Gross	F-G	6-6	200
14	Lionel Hollins	G	6-3	185
34	Robin Jones	F-C	6-9	225
20	Maurice Lucas	F-C	6-9	215
22	Clyde Mayes	F	6-8	225
36	Lloyd Neal	C-F	6-7	225
15	Larry Steele	G-F	6-5	180
13	Dave Twardzik	G	6-1	175
42	Wally Walker	F	6-7	190
32	Bill Walton	C-F	6-11	210

Team Stats

PTS	PPG	REB	RPG	AST	APG
9,163	111.7	3,963	48.3	1,990	24.3

Regular Season

49-33; Second Place – Pacific Division

Playoffs

Western Conference First Round:
Beat Chicago Bulls 2-1
Western Conference Semifinals:
Beat Denver Nuggets 4-2
Western Conference Finals:
Beat Los Angeles Lakers 4-0
NBA Finals: Beat Philadelphia 76ers 4-2

(Preceding page, and left) The 1976-77 Portland Trail Blazers. Front row (from left): Larry Weinberg (president), Harry Glickman (general manager), Herm Gilliam, Dave Twardzik, Johnny Davis, Lionel Hollins, Jack Ramsay (head coach), Jack McKinney (assistant coach). Middle row (from left): Lloyd Neal, Larry Steele, Corky Calhoun, Bill Walton, Maurice Lucas, Wally Walker, Robin Jones, Bob Gross. Back row (from left): Bill Schonley (radio announcer), Dr. Robert Cook (team physician), Ron Culp (trainer), Wallace Scales (promotions director), Dr. Larry Mudrick (team dentist), George Rickles (business manager), Berlyn Hodges (administrative assistant).

decades observing and commenting on the modern NBA. In 2011, Ramsay was asked if his 1976-77 Portland team was the best of all time.

"I don't know about that," he said, "but they could play with any team today."

In the 1977 playoffs, Walton and his teammates found a chemistry that enabled them to confuse and humiliate one of the most talented pro teams ever assembled, the Philadelphia 76ers led by Julius "Dr. J" Erving.

"Bill Walton is the best player, best competitor, best person I have ever coached," Ramsay would declare moments after Walton delivered Portland the NBA title.

That moment would prove to be the height of Walton's pro career, although he would come back from injury in 1986 to help the Celtics win a world championship as a backup center. But for the most part, his full pro potential was realized just once.

In college Walton kept his hair short to meet Wooden's team rules, but in Portland he grew his hair long and added a scraggly auburn beard. Still, he was the picture of passion and precision, schooled and polished in every phase of the game.

"He's another one of those who make all the players around him better," Wooden said of Walton.

His injuries emphasized that. He missed 17 games during the 1976-77 season. The Blazers lost 12 of them. With him in the lineup, they were 44-21, their .677 winning percentage during those games the best in the league. But no team's record was overwhelming.

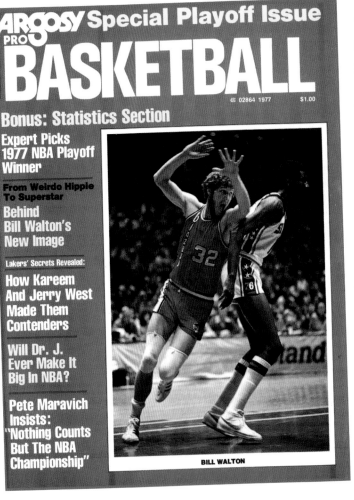

BILL WALTON

The ABA had folded after the 1975-76 season, and the redistribution of players from that league had resulted in greater parity, with six clubs getting at least 48 wins and another nine winning 40.

From the ABA, the Blazers nabbed Maurice Lucas, simply the most dominating power forward in the game, and his arrival only boosted Walton's effectiveness in the frontcourt. But Lucas' role was far from merely complimentary. He led the team in scoring at 20.2 points per game and averaged better than 11 rebounds.

His intimidation factor loomed even bigger than his numbers. At 6-foot-9 and a muscular 215 pounds, he wasn't the bulkiest player in the league — but he was almost the strongest. Because he played in Portland, the national media overlooked Lucas through much of the season. By April, though, his antics were in full view. Against the

(Preceding page) Walton (32) defends Philadelphia's Julius "Dr. J" Erving (6) during the 1977 NBA Finals as Portland's Lucas (20) waits for the result. Walton led the league in rebounds (14.4) and blocks (3.2) per game during the regular season, despite missing 17 games due to injury. He was selected as Finals MVP as he averaged 19.0 rebounds, 18.5 points, 5.2 assists and 3.7 blocks in the six-game victory over the 76ers. (Above) Walton's image changed from the mandated clean-cut ways at UCLA in college to free spirit in the NBA.

Ramsay wrapped this crew into a rebounding and running package that sent jolts through the Portland crowds. He was, after all, the thinking man's coach. In his past life, he had been the most respected of college coaches, molding wonderful teams at St. Joseph's in Philadelphia over 11 seasons.

Ramsay got his introduction to the pro game with the Buffalo Braves before taking over in Portland. In more than 20 seasons as an NBA coach, he would pile up 864 regular-season wins. But the 1976-77 season wasn't about regular-season wins. Because of the losses during Walton's absences, the Blazers finished 49-33, four games back of the Lakers in the Pacific Division. In the first round, Walton and company battled Artis Gilmore and the Chicago Bulls before winning a tough series 2-1. The next round brought a 4-2 dismissal of Denver, coached by Larry Brown. Portland simply offered too much running and too much rebounding for the Nuggets.

The Western Finals pitted the Blazers against the Lakers, which created a classic one-on-one matchup between Walton and his predecessor at UCLA, Kareem Abdul-Jabbar. Their meeting left the writers yodeling about future battles of Russell/Chamberlain proportions. The team contest, however, left a lot to be desired. The Lakers had been hit by heavy injuries, and Portland swept 4-0. The Blazers franchise was a mere seven seasons old and headed to the NBA Finals.

Their opponents would be the mercurial but awesomely talented Philadelphia 76ers, who had posted a 50-32 record, the best in the Eastern Conference. Gene Shue was the coach. Erving, forward George McGinnis and shooting guard Doug Collins were the big guns. The quarterback on the floor was point guard Henry Bibby. World B. Free rained long-range jumpers off the bench. And Caldwell Jones started at center with 21-year-old Darryl Dawkins, the self-proclaimed "Chocolate Thunder," in a backup role. As reserve forwards they had Steve Mix, Harvey Catchings and Joe Bryant.

On the whole, though, they were perceived as an undisciplined lot, beginning with the chain-smoking McGinnis and ending somewhere off in Lovetron, Dawkins' imaginary home planet.

In the last few months of the season, Erving and McGinnis had averaged 50 points per game together. The team started strongly as they downed Boston and Houston on the way to

Chicago Bulls in a brutal first-round playoff series, Lucas threw a strong jab at a team trainer and even jerked an official's whistle lariat.

Another ABA pickup, Dave Twardzik, ran the team with precision. The off guard was 6-foot-3 Lionel Hollins, in his second year out of Arizona State who averaged nearly 15 points a game. Veteran Herm Gilliam was the third guard and rookie Johnny Davis backed up Twardzik.

Bob Gross, 6-foot-6, in his second season out of Long Beach State, was the starting small forward and role player. He gave Ramsay 11.4 points and solid defense each game. And 6-foot-5 Larry Steele added 10.3 points in 20 minutes a game off the bench.

the Eastern Conference championship. Yet as the Finals opened in the Spectrum, few observers were convinced of the Sixers' resolve.

Philadelphia general manager Pat Williams acknowledged that the club was unpredictable. "But," he added, "we could win it all going away with our manes blowing in the wind."

That seemed to be just what was going to happen after the first two games. The Sixers won both at home, with the second game marked by an ugly bench-clearing brawl. In Game 1, Erving finished with 33 points, and Doug Collins had 30, as Philly won 107-101. And in Game 2 four nights later, the Sixers did an even better job, winning handily, 107-89.

But after the second game, Walton cut his hair and cleaned up his appearance. More importantly, the Blazers solved the riddle of the Sixers' deep talent and claimed the next four games in a whirlwind to grab the title. Commanding a 3-2 series lead, the Blazers had arrived home at 4:30 a.m. to find 5,000 crazy fans waiting to greet them. The official word for the mayhem was Blazermania.

Always an emotional player, Walton rode to new heights on the crest of this wave. The next afternoon, a glorious, sunny Sunday, he had 20 points, 23 rebounds, eight blocks and seven assists. "He's an inspiration," Erving would say afterward.

The Doctor himself wasn't bad in that department. His Sixers battled the entirety of Game 6, but only a second remained when McGinnis got a final shot. It drew iron, and that was it. Walton knocked away the loose ball just to be sure of the 109-107 victory, then turned, ripped off his drenched jersey and hurled it into the delirious crowd.

"If I had caught the shirt, I would have eaten it," Lucas allowed later. "Bill's my hero."

(Preceding page) Ramsay coached the Trail Blazers from a second-place divisional finish to an NBA title in 1976-77, as Portland won 14 of 19 playoff games. He was inducted into the Basketball Hall of Fame in 1992. (Right) Lucas (20) fires a jumper over the 76ers' George McGinnis (30) during the 1977 NBA Finals in Philadelphia. Lucas led the Blazers in scoring during the regular season (20.2 points per game) and playoffs (21.2).

ST. LOUIS HAWKS

1957-58 ST. LOUIS HAWKS

In his era, Bob Pettit epitomized basketball success. His statistics alone bear that out, although the numbers are only one indication of his greatness. Pettit's game was all about heart.

Like Michael Jordan years later, Pettit too was cut from his junior high team as a sophomore. But he made the varsity the following season after spending every spare minute he had at a backyard hoop.

Extra effort would become the hallmark of his career.

"When I fall below what I know I can do, my belly growls and growls," Pettit once said. This inability to digest mediocrity pushed him far beyond his talent.

"In his day, he was the best power forward that was," Red Auerbach said of Pettit. "Elgin Baylor was a close second.

1957-58 St. Louis Hawks

Coach: Alex Hannum

No.	Player	Pos.	Ht.	Wt.
11	Jack Coleman	F-C	6-7	195
12	Walt Davis	C-F	6-8	205
16	Cliff Hagan	F-G	6-4	210
20	Ed Macauley	C-F	6-8	185
22	Slater Martin	G	5-10	170
21	Jack McMahon	G	6-1	185
12	Red Morrison	F-C	6-8	220
17	Med Park	G-F	6-2	205
17	Worthy Patterson	G	6-2	175
9	Bob Pettit	F-C	6-9	205
19	Frank Selvy	G-F	6-3	180
13	Chuck Share	C	6-11	235
15	Win Wilfong	G-F	6-2	185

Team Stats

PTS	PPG	REB	RPG	AST	APG
7,738	107.5	5,445	75.6	1,541	21.4

Regular Season
41-31; First Place – Western Division

Playoffs
Western Division Finals:
    Beat Detroit Pistons 4-1
NBA Finals: Beat Boston Celtics 4-2

(Preceding page, and left) The 1957-58 St. Louis Hawks. Front row (from left): Alex Hannum (head coach), Cliff Hagan, Jack Coleman, Charlie Share (captain), Bob Pettit, Walt Davis, Ed Macauley. Back row (from left): Max Shapiro (ballboy), Slater Martin, Win Wilfong, Jack McMahon, Med Park, Frank Selvy, Bernie Ebert (trainer).

He was drafted by the Milwaukee Hawks in 1954, but found that he couldn't outmuscle Charlie Share at center and was moved to forward. For the first time in his career, he had to play facing the basket. Pettit worked overtime to adjust his game. He became a starter for coach Red Holzman's Hawks, but the other forwards in the league had their turns at teaching him lessons. Vern Mikkelsen of the Minneapolis Lakers overpowered him. Dolph Schayes of the Syracuse Nationals befuddled him with slick offense. Maurice Stokes of the Cincinnati Royals moved around him with superior quickness. But Pettit eventually found a way to counter all of them.

He averaged 20.4 points his first season (fourth best in the league) and finished third in rebounding. That performance earned him Rookie of the Year and presaged his stardom. He made the All-NBA first team for 10 of the 11 years he played. In 1956, he became one of only three players in NBA history to lead the league in both rebounding and scoring. (He retired in 1965 as the leading scorer in NBA history, although he knew the record wouldn't last long with Wilt Chamberlain in the league.).

"He kept coming at you," Schayes said. "There was no way you could stop him over the course of a game. He was just too strong."

The Hawks moved to St. Louis after Pettit's rookie season, and he soon became the favorite of crowds there. He came to be known as "Big Blue" because of his insistence on wearing a ratty old blue overcoat.

That affection increased during the height of Pettit's career from 1957-61, when he led the Hawks to four NBA Finals. Only once, in 1958, did they claim the trophy, losing the other three times to the Boston Celtics. Yet the effort was enough to establish St. Louis as one of the best clubs in league history. And although the franchise later moved to Atlanta, the Hawks' 1958 championship still stirs hearts in St. Louis.

The 1957-58 season was one in a chain of Pettit's outstanding campaigns. He averaged 24.6 points and 17.4 rebounds per game while boosting the Hawks to the Western Division crown with a 41-31 record.

Pettit could do more things than Baylor, because he could play some center. And he was a better rebounder than Baylor. ... He would play all out, whether he was 50 points ahead or 50 behind. It didn't matter. That's the only way he knew how to play — all out."

Pettit entered college at LSU as an unsung 6-foot-7 player. But Pettit grew into a 6-foot-9 center and retained his mobility. He averaged 27.4 points per game over his college career, outstanding numbers in the era of slower basketball and good enough to make Pettit a three-time All-American.

(Top left) Hawks top guard Martin averaged 12.0 points per game during the 1957-58 regular season. (Opposite page) Pettit (9) goes in for a layup during a home game in St. Louis. Pettit's strong inside play as a scorer and rebounder helped the Hawks play in four NBA championship series in five years from 1957-61. In St. Louis' lone title season of 1957-58, he averaged 24.6 points and 17.4 rebounds.

By no means, though, were the Hawks a one-man team. Both Jack McMahon and Hall of Famer Slater Martin gave St. Louis an excellent set of ball-pressure guards who knew how to direct the offense to Pettit.

To go with this backcourt, the Hawks still had smooth-shooting "Easy Ed" Macauley, Chuck Share and Jack Coleman in the frontcourt.

Also there was 6-foot-4 small forward Cliff Hagan, the team's other major point producer, averaging 19.9 points per game while shooting .443 from the floor, second best in the league. Despite his height, Hagan found a way to post up and dominate inside.

"He was the Adrian Dantley of his day," Auerbach said, comparing Hagan to one of his favorite players of the 1980s. "He played the game the same way. He was a very powerful man. And a proud man."

Hagan had begun perfecting his inside moves as a high school center in Owensboro, Kentucky. He joined the Celtics' Frank Ramsey at the University of Kentucky, where they starred on three of coach Adolph Rupp's best teams. Hagan had a wonderful hook shot and a rebounding fierceness that earned him consensus All-America honors in 1951-52. "When Hagan took a hook shot, I knew that thing was going in," Ramsey said of his teammate.

Drawing their strength from these talents, the Hawks blasted the Pistons 4-1 in the Western Division Finals and advanced to the championship series for the second consecutive year. They had lost the 1957 title to the Celtics in a wild seven-game series that ended with Boston leading by 2 points in overtime with almost no time left on the clock. St. Louis player/coach Alex Hannum had to

(Left) Hagan (16) defends Cincinnati's Jack Twyman (27) in an early 1960s game in St. Louis. Hagan, despite playing taller opponents, led the Hawks in scoring during the 1958 playoffs, averaging 27.7 points, better than Pettit's 24.2 average.

inbound the ball the length of the court and planned to bank the pass off the backboard in the hope that Pettit could tip it in. Incredibly, Hannum banked the pass off the board to Pettit, but the final shot rolled off the rim.

From that heartache, Pettit was on fire for another shot at Bill Russell and the Celtics. For 1958, Boston had dominated the Eastern Division with a 49-23 record. Russell led the league in rebounding with the unheard of average of 22.7 per game. Hall of Fame guard Bill Sharman led them in scoring with a 22.3 average. And Auerbach had added his newest weapon, Sam Jones, a surprise first-round pick in the draft, out of little North Carolina Central. In time, Jones would become a Hall of Famer. But for the present, he fit in nicely coming off the Boston bench.

With Bob Cousy leading the league in assists (7.1 per game), Boston ran past Syracuse to win the Eastern Division title by eight games. The players had voted Russell the league MVP, but the writers placed him on the All-NBA second team.

Later, after St. Louis vanquished Boston, many observers figured the Celtics probably would have won the 1958 title if Russell hadn't suffered an ankle injury in the third game of the series. Auerbach, however, disputed that opinion.

"You can always look for excuses," he said in 1990. "We just got beat."

The results support that conclusion. The Hawks upset the Celtics 104-102 with a healthy Russell in Game 1 in Boston Garden. Boston cracked back with a 136-112 wipeout in Game 2. Back in St. Louis, the Hawks held serve 111-108 in Game 3 when Russell injured his ankle. Then, without Russell, the Celtics evened the series with a 109-98 surprise in Game 4. Still, Boston was drastically undermanned in the frontcourt. Jim Loscutoff had missed the entire season with an injury, and Russell's bad ankle left only Tom Heinsohn and graybeard Arnie Risen to deal with the Hawks' power game. Even so, it was no cakewalk. St. Louis forced a 102-100 win in Boston Garden to take a 3-2 lead.

Back home in Kiel Auditorium on April 12, the Hawks weren't about to miss their opportunity. Pettit guaranteed that, turning in a solidly spectacular performance. He scored 31 points in the first three quarters, then he zoomed off in the final period, nailing 19 of his team's last 21 points, as the Celtics fouled repeatedly, trying to stop him. His last basket, a tip-in with 15 seconds remaining, put the Hawks ahead 110-107. The Celtics scored a meaningless bucket and could do no more. Pettit's team finally had a title with the 110-109 victory.

Pettit's 50-point performance tied the single-game playoff scoring record set by Cousy against Syracuse in 1953. But Cousy's record had been set in a four-overtime game, an event so foul-plagued that he hit 30 of his points from the free-throw line. Pettit's 50-point performance was stunning. Better yet, it had delivered his team the title, just the kind of effort Hawks fans had come to expect from "Big Blue."

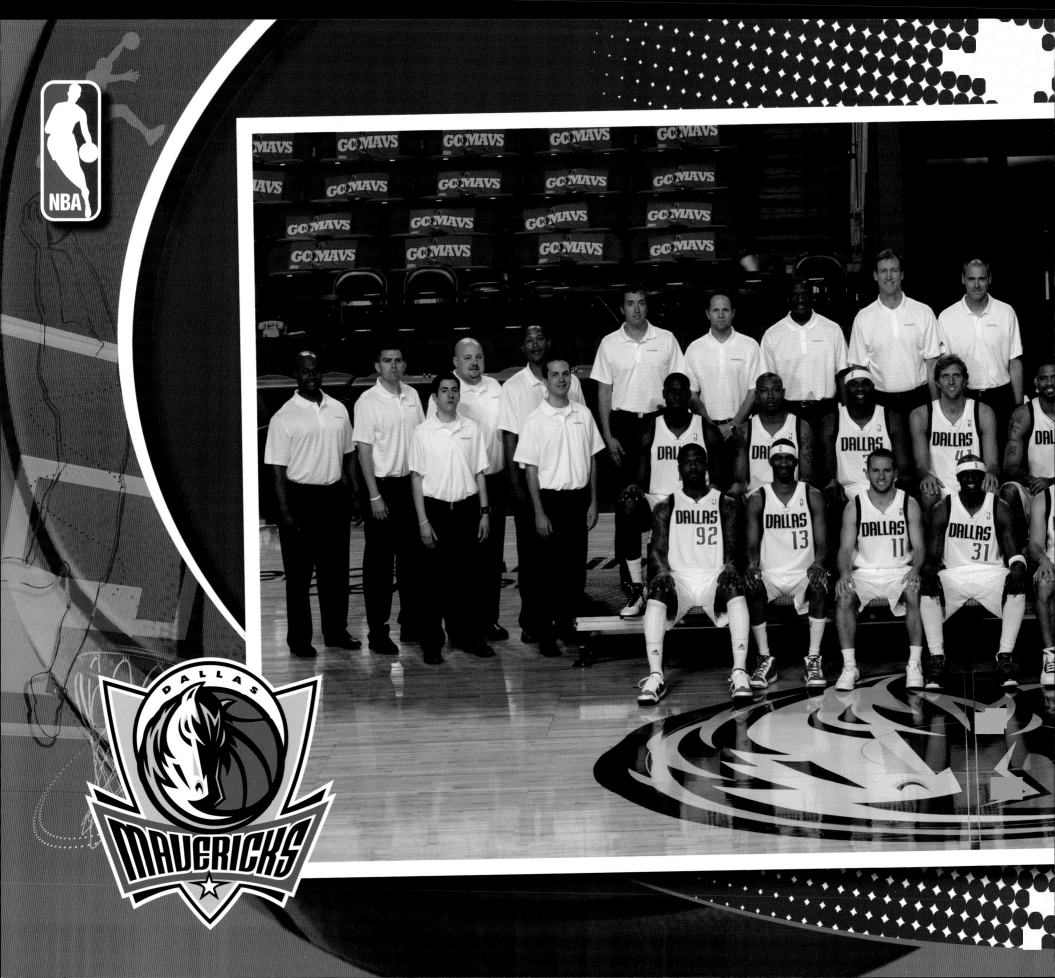

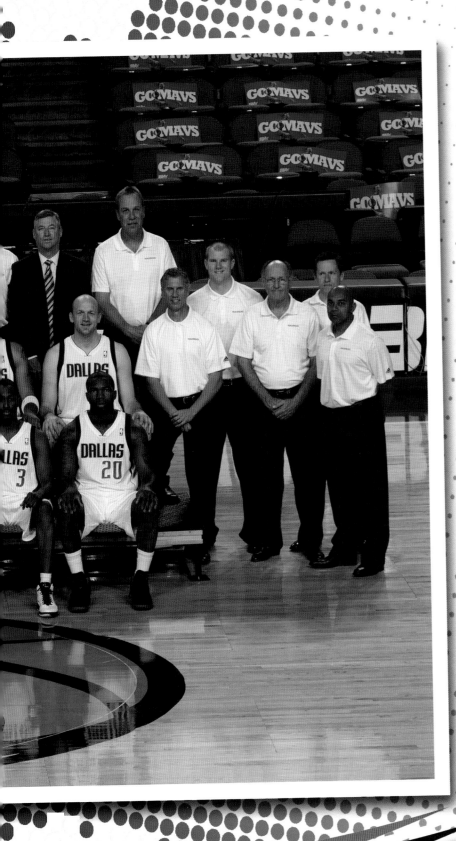

2010-11 DALLAS MAVERICKS

Phil Jackson was one of the first to see the rise of the Dallas Mavericks, but he didn't broadcast it. He just mentioned it to a friend early in the 2010-2011 NBA season.

Having coached the Chicago Bulls and Los Angeles Lakers to 11 NBA titles, Jackson had earned his reputation as a master of matchups. He always looked around early in the season and sized up the opposition.

The Dallas Mavericks are a team to be reckoned with, Jackson hinted privately in late 2010.

(Preceding page, and left) The 2010-11 Dallas Mavericks. Front row (from left): DeShawn Stevenson, Corey Brewer, Jose Barea, Jason Terry, Jason Kidd, Rodrigue Beaubois, Dominique Jones. Middle row (from left): Ian Mahinmi, Caron Butler, Brendan Haywood, Dirk Nowitzki, Tyson Chandler, Shawn Marion, Brian Cardinal. Back row (from left): Dionne Calhoun (assistant athletic trainer), Mike Weinar (special assistant), Neil Herskowitz (assistant equipment manager), Mike Shedd (head video coordinator/scout), Mondrick Jones (video scout), Terry Sullivan (video scout), Casey Smith (head athletic trainer), Monte Mathis (assistant coach), Dwane Casey (assistant coach), Terry Stotts (assistant coach), Rick Carlisle (head coach), Donnie Nelson (general manager), Darrell Armstrong (assistant coach), Keith Grant (assistant GM), Brad Davis (player development coach), Don Kalkstein (director of sport psychology), Al Whitley (equipment manager), Gary Boren (free throw coach), Roland Beech (director of basketball analytics), Robert Hackett (assistant coach/ strength and conditioning).

2010-11 Dallas Mavericks

Coach: Rick Carlisle

No.	Player	Pos.	Ht.	Wt.
8	Alexis Ajinca	C	7-0	220
11	Jose Barea	G	6-0	175
3	Rodrigue Beaubois	G	6-0	170
13	Corey Brewer	F	6-9	185
4	Caron Butler	F	6-7	217
35	Brian Cardinal	F	6-8	245
6	Tyson Chandler	C	7-1	235
33	Brendan Haywood	C	7-0	268
20	Dominique Jones	G	6-4	215
2	Jason Kidd	G	6-4	205
28	Ian Mahinmi	C	6-11	230
0	Shawn Marion	F	6-7	220
21	Steve Novak	F	6-10	220
41	Dirk Nowitzki	F	7-0	237
7	Sasha Pavlovic	G-F	6-8	220
92	DeShawn Stevenson	G	6-5	210
16	Peja Stojakovic	F-G	6-9	220
31	Jason Terry	G	6-2	176

Team Stats

PTS	PPG	REB	RPG	AST	APG
8,220	100.2	3,398	41.4	1,954	23.8

Regular Season
57-25; Second Place – Southwest Division

Playoffs
Western Conference First Round:
Beat Portland Trail Blazers 4-2
Western Conference Semifinals:
Beat Los Angeles Lakers 4-0
Western Conference Finals:
Beat Oklahoma City Thunder 4-1
NBA Finals: Beat Miami Heat 4-2

His prediction raised eyebrows, even among friends. The same Dallas Mavericks who had blown a 2-0 lead in the 2006 NBA Finals? The same Mavs who had made a first-round playoff exit in three of the four previous seasons? The Dallas team owned by Mark Cuban, who spares no expense but seems to always somehow screw the pooch?

Exactly.

Jackson mentioned that small forward Caron Butler, who came to Dallas during the 2009-10 season, was the reason for his concern. Now that Dallas had a top-notch small forward, they would be tough to handle, Jackson said.

Not long after Jackson made his comments, Butler was lost for the season to a knee injury.

It says much about the 2010-11 Mavericks that they survived the loss of Butler and found a way to make their mark in history.

"This is a special team," Mavericks coach Rick Carlisle said of his club after they defeated the favored Miami Heat for the 2011 title. "This is the most special team that I've ever been around, because it's not about what you can't do; it's about what you can do. It's not about what your potential shortcomings are; it's what we could accomplish as a group together."

On the way to claiming the title, Carlisle's team pushed aside Jackson's two-time defending champions — in a four-game sweep in the Western Conference playoffs.

Only in retrospect did Jackson's prediction make perfect sense. The Mavericks were led by the great Jason Kidd at point guard. Yes, he was 37 years old when the season began, but he had matured with age and made himself into an offensive threat (better than 40 percent on 3-pointers) after years as a master passer with no shot.

Above all, he was also one of the game's all-time competitors with tremendous court vision and game smarts. Twice Kidd had led the New Jersey Nets to the NBA Finals only to lose. He lived for a title.

The cliché is that a point guard has to be the coach on the floor. Kidd literally was the coach. Carlisle talked repeatedly about how

much he learned about the game from Kidd, no small comment in that Carlisle was already a veteran coach when he arrived in Dallas.

"I've learned so much from these guys," Carlisle would point out. "Especially Jason Kidd. His view of the game is so different, and he's savant like."

Jackson, though, was also talking matchups in his appraisal of Dallas, and Mavs power forward Dirk Nowitzki would emphasize

(Preceding page) Terry (31) drives past Miami's Eddie House (55) for 2 of his 27 points during the clinching Game 6 of the 2011 NBA Finals in Miami. Terry averaged 18 points during the Finals over the Heat. (Top right) Carlisle encourages his team from the bench during Game 6 of the 2011 NBA Finals. Carlisle, who was part of the 1986 champion Boston Celtics as a player, coached the Mavericks to their first NBA title.

in 2011 something that his career performances had long suggested — he was the ultimate mismatch nightmare for opponents.

Nowitzki, who had re-signed with the Mavs over the summer of 2010 for a reported $80 million over four years, had long been the team's offensive engine. In 2009-10 he had finished seventh in the league in scoring at 25 points a game, in addition to 7.7 rebounds, 48.1 percent from the field, 42.1 percent on 3-point shots and second in the league in free-throw accuracy — just the kind of performance he had turned in year-in and year-out.

In the 2010-11 regular season, those numbers slipped to 23 points and seven rebounds, but that was a sign that Nowitzki had more help.

In particular, he had center Tyson Chandler, who upgraded a Mavs roster that finished 15th in shooting defense and 24th in rebounding percentage in 2009-10. Chandler was the starting center on Team USA's 2008 Olympic gold-medal unit, a tremendous confidence booster. He too had matured into the kind of tough guy in the post, something that Dallas had lacked for years, something that had hindered Nowitzki's development as he was required to play both the four and five positions.

"He knows what he can do and does it well," Lakers assistant coach Tex Winter, who had studied Nowitzki closely, observed in 2008. "The situation he's been in in Dallas, it's been difficult to define a definite position for him because their centers have been so lacking. (He) has had to play the five both defensively and offensively at times. That has taken away from his effectiveness."

Also huge were the lingering burns from 2006. Nowitzki and super sixth man Jason "Jet" Terry were left from the Mavs team that had taken a 2-0 lead over the Heat in the NBA Finals, only to be swept in four straight.

"Dirk and Jet have had to live for five years with what happened in 2006," Carlisle would explain.

To up the ante on that old heartbreak, Terry had the Larry O'Brien NBA Championship Trophy tattooed on his right bicep before the 2011 season, a measure of his confidence that the Mavs would finally claim the title. However, his 15.8 points per game off the bench were far more valuable than any tattoo.

There were many other major factors, starting with Shawn Marion, the once highly valued "Matrix," finding his comfort zone as a first-rate role player in Dallas who averaged 12.5 points and 6.9 rebounds in 2011. Marion could defend and could also play power forward in a small lineup, tremendous versatility.

Veterans DeShawn Stevenson and Peja Stojakovic also found roles and played them well.

If you have a 37-year-old point guard, you better have depth, and the Mavs had plenty of that with Jose Barea and Rodrigue Beaubois. Barea, in particular, played a larger role as the Mavs came alive in the 2011 playoffs, despite his size (6-feet, 175 pounds).

But it was the old standards, Nowitzki and Terry, who truly jumped their games up in the playoffs. Nowitzki pushed his scoring to 27.7 a game and Terry to 17.5 as the pressure hit the high side.

They allowed the Mavs to present matchup headaches for their playoff opponents. After a shaky start, they ditched Portland 4-2 in the first round. Then came their blasting of Los Angeles in the conference semifinals and with it their confidence grew.

The young, talented, athletic Oklahoma City Thunder fell 4-1 in the conference finals, and the immediate talk turned to how quickly LeBron James, Dwyane Wade and the Miami Heat would dismiss Dallas in the NBA Finals.

It looked like a sweep as the Heat won Game 1 in Miami and made Game 2 look like a shoe commercial of slam dunks and breakaways for almost three quarters.

But Nowitzki led a rousing and strange comeback in Game 2 that allowed Dallas to tie the series. Then it became of matter of the Mavericks' superior offense finding the moxie to wear out Miami's defense.

That's exactly what happened as Dallas claimed the title on Miami's home floor 105-95 in Game 6.

"This is one of the unique teams in NBA history," Carlisle, who had also won a championship ring as a player with the Boston Celtics, observed afterward. "Because it wasn't about high-flying star power. ... When are people going to talk about the purity of our game and what these guys accomplished? That's what's special. And I played with Larry Bird, I played with Bill Walton, I played with Robert Parish, I played with Dennis Johnson. I played with the all-time greats. And Dirk is up there with that upper, upper echelon of great players. He's arguably one of the most unique players in the history of the game. Because there's never been a 7-foot player that has developed his skill and his resourcefulness for being able to find ways to score."

Terry, too, had more than shown his worth with 27 points in the clinching win over Miami.

"When you did something as crazy as I did, you have to back it up," Terry said after the game as he showed his tattoo to the television cameras. "This team never gave up when faced with adversity. We never gave up. Tonight we got vindication."

(Preceding page) Nowitzki shoots a 3-pointer during Game 6 of the 2011 NBA Finals against the Miami Heat. The Mavericks' star was named the Finals MVP after averaging 26 points and 9.7 rebounds in the six games against the Heat. Dallas won its first NBA title after 31 seasons of play.

A great basketball team has to have several things to succeed. First, they need a deep passion and intense desire to win. Then they must have a high level of basketball intellect and understand how the game is played at both ends of the floor. Every player has to understand their role to maximize their skills and talents.

Great teams also have great leaders, just like within any organization or system. These leaders understand the team vision, goals and objectives, and through their words and actions they influence their teammates on the court and off.

Inside the pages of *The NBA's Greatest Teams* book, author and NBA observer Roland Lazenby talks about 20 great teams, their star players, their role players and their coaches who came together for 20 special seasons during the history of the NBA.

Great teams usually have two or three tremendous players but they also have players who epitomize teamwork and sacrifice, who defend when they have to defend, and who have an indomitable competitive drive and a great will to win

Role players on great teams are critical and there is no success without them. When you look at all the teams in this book, the best role players sacrificed for the good of the team as they worked their tails off trying to win a championship.

Of course, the coaching staff of every great team has to juggle the egos and competitive nature of every player, and within these pages are some of the great coaches in the history of the NBA. Coaching is not easy and the coaching staffs who win championships do an amazing job over the course of a long season.

When you stack up the teams in this book, they are all impressive. Each one did the little things they had to do to compete. Players understood their roles and sacrificed accordingly, and the great ones rose to the occasion. Michael Jordan, Magic Johnson, Bill Russell, Bill Walton, Oscar Robertson, Moses Malone, Julius Erving and Larry Bird were just some of the greats who willed their teams to victory.

I played against five teams on this list during my career: the 1970-71 Milwaukee Bucks, the 1971-72 Los Angeles Lakers, the 1973-74 Boston Celtics, the 1976-77 Portland Trail Blazers and the 1982-83 Philadelphia 76ers. Each of those teams had all the ingredients along with the drive and the talent to be the best.

Which NBA team is the greatest of all time? Even when the Basketball Hall of Famers get together, we can't agree. As my good friend Bill Russell would always say, "You can talk all you want about anybody and all these teams, but I just want you to know, I have 10 fingers and 11 rings — my case is closed."

— Bob Lanier
Detroit Pistons 1970-80,
Milwaukee Bucks 1980-84
Basketball Hall of Famer (Class of 1992)

About The Author

Roland Lazenby has written extensively about the NBA over the years, including *Jerry West, The Life And Legend Of A Basketball Icon*, published in 2010 by ESPN Books, which was called by the *Los Angeles Times* a "first-rate piece of narrative non-fiction." His works include several titles about the Lakers, including *The Show*, an oral history of the Lakers; *Mad Game*, a biography of Kobe Bryant; *The Lakers, A Basketball Journey*; and *Mindgames*, a biography of Phil Jackson. During the Larry Bird era in Boston, Lazenby wrote and produced five editions of the *Boston Celtics Greenbook*. Lazenby has also written the history of the NBA Finals, and is the longtime editor of *Lindy's Pro Basketball Annual*. He lives in the Blue Ridge Mountains of Virginia with his wife Karen. Their children are Jenna, Henry and Morgan.

Acknowledgments

I would like to thank the folks at Whitman Publishing, who have done an outstanding job on this project. Also, the compilation of this book would not have been possible without the front-line work of a variety of reporters and writers over the years. That group includes the following:

J.A. Adande, Mitch Albom, David Aldridge, Jim Alexander, Elliott Almond, Neil Amdur, Dave Anderson, Howard Beck, Ira Berkow, Steve Bisheff, Greg Boeck, Mike Bresnahan, Cliff Brown, Tim Brown, Ric Bucher, Bryan Burwell, Kelly Carter, E. Jean Carroll, Mitch Chortkoff, Marlene Cimons, Doug Cress, Karen Crouse, Tim Deady, Frank DeFord, Kevin Ding, David Dupree, Larry Donald, Mike Downey, Ron Dungee, Melvin Durslag, David Ferrell, Joe Fitzgerald, Mal Florence, John Freeman, Tom Friend, Bud Furillo, Frank Girardot, Sam Goldaper, Brian Golden, Alan Goldstein, Ted Green, Allen Greenberg, Don Greenberg, Milton Gross, Donald Hall, Merv Harris, Randy Harvey, Mark Heisler, Steve Henson, Randy Hill, Bruce Horovitz, Scott Howard-Cooper, Mary Ann Hudson, Bob Hunter, Michael Hurd, Doug Ives, Bruce Jenkins, Roy S. Johnson, William Oscar Johnson, Tim Kawakami, Dave Kindred, Doug Krikorian, Leonard Koppett, Tony Kornheiser, Doug Krikorian, Rich Levin, Bill Libby, Mike Littwin, Leonard Lewin, Jack Madden, Allan Malamud, Jack McCallum, Sam McManis, Jackie MacMullen, John L. Mitchell, Kevin Modesti, David Leon Moore, Morton Moss, Bruce Newman, Scott Ostler, Sandy Padwe, Chris Palmer, John Papanek, Charles Pierce, Bill Plaschke, Diane Pucin, Pat Putnam, Brad Pye Jr., Ron Rapoport, Bob Ryan, Steve Springer, Bill Steigerwald, Marc Stein, Larry Stewart, Eric Tracy, Brad Turner, Michael Ventre, George Vecsey, Peter Vecsey, Lesley Visser, Mike Waldner, Peter Warner, Mark Whicker and Alex Wolff.

Photo Credits

All photos credited to NBAE/Getty Images.

Bibliography

A number of excellent books and periodicals provided me with background for this project.

Newspapers and Magazines

Extensive use was made of a variety of publications, including *AirCal, Basketball Times, Boston Globe, Boston Herald, Business Week, Chicago Tribune, Chicago Sun-Times, The Detroit News, Detroit Free Press, ESPN The Magazine, Esquire, Flint Journal, Forbes, GQ, Hartford Courant, Hoop Magazine, Houston Post, Let's Talk!, Los Angeles Business Journal, Los Angeles Daily News, Los Angeles Lakers Illustrated, Los Angeles Times, Los Angeles Herald-Examiner, Lindy's Pro Basketball Annual, Los Angeles Sentinel, The National, New York Daily News, The New York Times, New York Post, New West, The Oakland Press, The Roanoke Times & World-News, The Charlotte Observer, USA Today, Vanity Fair, The Orange County Register, The Philadelphia Inquirer, San Diego Tribune, Sport, Sports Illustrated, The Sporting News, Street & Smith's Pro Basketball Yearbook* and *The Washington Post*.

Books

- *24 Seconds to Shoot* by Leonard Koppett, Macmillan, New York, 1980.
- *50 Years of the Final Four* by Billy Packer and Roland Lazenby, Taylor Publishing, Dallas, 1987.
- *100 Greatest Basketball Players* by Wayne Patterson and Lisa Fisher, Bison Books, Greenwich, Conn., 1988.
- *100 Years of Hoops* by Alexander Wolff, Oxmoor House, Birmingham, 1992.
- *A Dangerous Place* by Marc Reisner, Pantheon Books, New York 2003.
- *A View From Above* by Wilt Chamberlain, Signet Books, 1992.
- *Bad Boys* by Isiah Thomas and Matt Dobek, Masters Press, Grand Rapids, 1989.
- *Basketball My Way* by Jerry West with Bill Libby, Prentice-Hall, Englewood Cliffs, 1973.
- *Basketball's Greatest Games* edited by Zander Hollander, Prentice Hall, Englewood Cliffs, 1971.
- *Basketball's Hall of Fame* by Sandy Padwe, Grossett and Dunlap, New York, 1973.
- *Cages to Jump Shots* by Robert Peterson, Oxford, 1990.
- *Championship NBA* by Leonard Koppett, Dial Press, New York, 1970.
- *Clown* by Bill Libby, Cowles Book Co., New York, 1970.
- *Coach* by Ray Meyer and Ray Sons, Contemporary, Chicago, 1987.
- *College Basketball's 25 Greatest Teams* by Billy Packer and Roland Lazenby, The Sporting News, St. Louis, 1989.
- *From Set Shot to Slam Dunk* by Charles Salzberg, Dutton, New York, 1987.
- *Gail Goodrich's Winning Basketball* by Gail Goodrich and Rich Levin, Contemporary, Chicago, 1976.
- *Giant Steps* by Kareem Abdul-Jabbar and Peter Knobler, Bantam, New York, 1983.
- *Giants* by Mark Heisler and Roland Lazenby, Triumph Books, Chicago, 2003.
- *Holtzman on Hoops* by Red Holtzman and Harvey Frommer, Taylor, Dallas, 1991.
- *Horny Los Angeles* edited by Jessica Hundley and Jon Alain Guzik, Really Great Books, Los Angeles, 2001.
- *Kareem* by Kareem Abdul-Jabbar and Mignon McCarthy, Random House, New York, 1990.
- *Lakers* by Joseph Hession, Foghorn Press, 1994.
- *Los Angeles: Biography Of A City* edited by John and Laree Caughey, University of California Press, 1977.
- *Magic's Touch* by Magic Johnson and Roy S. Johnson, Addison Wesley, Boston, 1989.
- *March to the Top* by Art Chansky and Eddie Fogler, Four Corners Press, Chapel Hill, 1982.
- *Miracle on 34th Street* by Phil Berger, Simon and Schuster, New York, 1970.
- *Mr. Clutch* by Jerry West and Bill Libby, Prentice-Hall, Englewood Cliffs, 1969.
- *My Life* by Earvin Johnson and William Novak, Random House, New York, 1992.
- *Magic* by Earvin Johnson and Rich Levine, Viking, New York, 1983.
- *Pro Basketball Champions* by George Vecsey, Scholastic, New York, 1970.
- *Rick Barry's Pro Basketball Scouting Report* by Rick Barry and Jordan E. Cohn, Bonus Books, Chicago, 1989.
- *Second Wind: The Memoirs of an Opinionated Man* by Bill Russell and Taylor Branch, Random House, New York, 1979.
- *Showtime* by Pat Riley and Byron Laursen, Warner Books, New York, 1987.
- *Sportswit* by Lee Green, Fawcett, New York, 1986.
- *Tall Tales* by Terry Pluto, Simon and Schuster, New York, 1992.
- *The Bird Era* by Bob Schron and Kevin Stevens, Quinland Press, Boston, 1988.
- *The Breaks of the Game* by David Halberstam, Knopf, New York, 1981.
- *The Glory and the Dream* by William Manchester, Little, Brown, Boston, 1974.
- *The Golden Boys* by Cameron Stauth, Pocket Books, New York, 1992.
- *The History of Professional Basketball Since 1896* by Glenn Dickey, Stein and Day, New York, 1982.
- *The Jim Murray Collection* by Jim Murray, Taylor Publishing, Dallas, 1989.
- *The Lakers* by Jack Clary, Brompton Books, 1992.
- *The Lakers: A Basketball Journey* by Roland Lazenby, St. Martin's Press, New York, 1993.
- *The Legend of Dr. J* by Marty Bell, New American Library, New York, 1981.
- *The Lives of Riley* by Mark Heisler, MacMillan, New York, 1994.
- *The Los Angeles Times Encyclopedia of the Lakers* by Steve Springer, The Los Angeles Times, 1998.
- *The Modern Basketball Encyclopedia* by Zander Hollander, Dolphin, Garden City, N.Y., 1979.
- *The NBA Finals* by Roland Lazenby, Taylor Publishing, Dallas, 1990.
- *The Night Wilt Scored 100* by Eric Nadel, Taylor Publishing, Dallas, 1990.
- *The Official NBA Basketball Encyclopedia* edited by Zander Hollander and Alex Sachare, Villard, New York, 1989.
- *The Sports Encyclopedia, Pro Basketball* by David S. Neft and Richard M. Cohen, St. Martin's Press, New York, 1992.
- *The Story of Basketball* by Dave Anderson, New York, 1989.
- *They Call Me Coach* by John Wooden and Jack Tobin, Word, Waco, Texas, 1972.
- *Walt Frazier* by Walt Frazier and Neil Offen, Times Books, New York, 1988.
- *Winnin' Times* by Scott Ostler and Steve Springer, Macmillan, New York, 1986.
- *Wilt* by Wilt Chamberlain and David Shaw, Macmillan, New York, 1986.

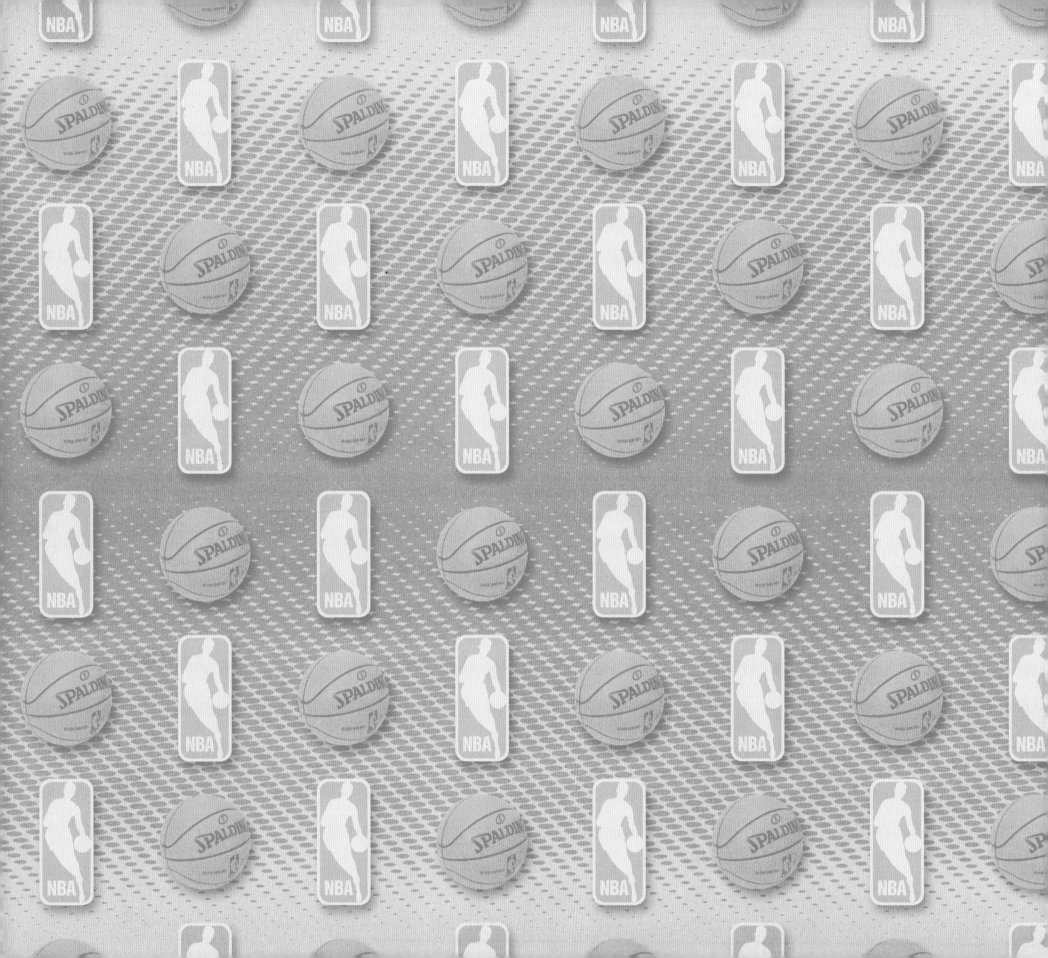